the daily happiness multiplier

the daily
happiness
multiplier

52 Secret Habits to Discover
Your True Hidden Potential
in Life and Business

Bimal Shah

New York

the daily happiness multiplier
52 Secret Habits to Discover Your True Hidden Potential in Life and Business

© 2016 Bimal Shah.

Published in New York, New York, by Morgan James Publishing. Morgan James and The Entrepreneurial Publisher are trademarks of Morgan James, LLC.
www.MorganJamesPublishing.com

The Morgan James Speakers Group can bring authors to your live event. For more information or to book an event visit The Morgan James Speakers Group at www.TheMorganJamesSpeakersGroup.com.

Always consult an attorney or tax professional or your financial advisor regarding your specific legal or tax or financial situation.

In addition, Information in this book do not involve the rendering of personalized health or fitness advice. A healthcare professional or your personal physician should be consulted for your needs. No content should not be construed as health or medical advice. Always consult a doctor or health care professional regarding your specific medical or health situation. Any inference or content or information to any fitness or exercise should not be construed as any fitness advice. A fitness expert should be consulted for your fitness needs.

Shelfie

A free eBook edition is available with the purchase of this print book.

CLEARLY PRINT YOUR NAME ABOVE IN UPPER CASE

Instructions to claim your free eBook edition:
1. Download the Shelfie app for Android or iOS
2. Write your name in **UPPER CASE** above
3. Use the Shelfie app to submit a photo
4. Download your eBook to any device

ISBN 978-1-63047-599-4 paperback
ISBN 978-1-63047-601-4 eBook
ISBN 978-1-63047-600-7 hardcover
Library of Congress Control Number:
2015935923

Cover Design by:
Chris Treccani
www.3dogdesign.net

Interior Design by:
Bonnie Bushman
The Whole Caboodle Graphic Design

In an effort to support local communities and raise awareness and funds, Morgan James Publishing donates a percentage of all book sales for the life of each book to Habitat for Humanity Peninsula and Greater Williamsburg

Get involved today, visit
www.MorganJamesBuilds.com

Habitat
for Humanity®
Peninsula and
Greater Williamsburg
Building Partner

Dedicated to my wife Ami and two daughters, Rajvi and Parthvi. This book wouldn't have been possible without the relentless efforts of my wife Ami on the editing, and the insights from my lovely daughters. They have been with me through this roller coaster ride and I love you all from the bottom of my heart.

contents

"Happiness is in all of us and true happiness comes from progress of inner personal and professional development.

The root cause of our development or destruction lies inside of us. The continued and persistent efforts we make on a daily basis on our own development leads to multiplication of the happiness in us on a daily basis. That's what makes us unique and gives us the reason for our existence."

—Bimal Shah

"I am on a Mission to provide security from enemies of prosperity and build one million daily high performers. I do it by building and maintaining customized systems of coaching, planning, and accountability."

—Bimal Shah

the human struggle for happiness

Happiness, nothing so enigmatic has been pursued for so long and with such passion by humans who have been willing to start revolutions and drive civilizations to their ruin for the sake of achieving it. Meanwhile philosophers, religious leaders, scientists, psychologists, and even politicians have spent centuries on defining what "it" is? And, to this day, there is no more clarity on the meaning of happiness. Aristotle, the great philosopher proclaimed it as the "ultimate purpose of human existence." The pursuit of happiness still consumes the lives of every human being on the planet. After all, who doesn't want to be happy? Yet, if the research is to be believed, it still seems to escape most of us.

The real question is, how do you, personally, define happiness; and, if you could define it, would you know how to purposely achieve it; then, would you even know happiness if you achieved it?

We all experience moments of happiness – the warmth of another human being, the joy of a puppy, the extra bonus in a paycheck, the birth of a child. In one sense, happiness is all around us; but so is the weather; and it can change from good to bad in an instant. The moments that bring us happiness can evaporate in an instant, replaced by periods of darkness that can bring despair. Can happiness even be controlled?

Aristotle, who actually introduced the "science of happiness," concluded that, in order to achieve true happiness, we must depend on ourselves. He was convinced that genuine happiness required the realization of a number of conditions that shaped our physical and mental well-being; not limited to material things, but that involved the cultivation of virtue over our lifetimes. As the "ultimate purpose of human existence," a true state-of-happiness is not a quest, but, rather an end which is desirable for the sake of itself, not for the sake of something or someone else.

Translated into today's terms, happiness cannot be achieved through possessions or even cumulative moments of joy; rather, it is the culmination of a purposeful journey with complete self-fulfillment as the final destination. Perhaps, that is why happiness is so elusive for so many.

Happiness is too often measured by what we have or how we feel, here and now versus what we hope to achieve through a lifetime dedicated to purpose. The reality is that, too many people go through life without a purpose – knowing what it is that can bring them true happiness.

In the modern world, especially in this country, happiness is typically equated with the feeling of well-being at any given moment. But, if all it took was a cold beer on a hot summer day, or, for the hardcore among us, a shot of drug, to create a feeling of well-being, happiness could only be measured in terms of minutes or hours versus a lifetime. Aristotle believed that genuine happiness could only be measured after a lifetime of accomplishment.

Does that mean we can't know happiness until late in life? Not necessarily. In life, as in any kind of journey, if you know your destination, and you know you're on the right path to that destination, each step along the way brings an increment of fulfillment. As long as we are advancing towards the goals we want to achieve, we can enjoy happiness. Without a life destination – a defined purpose or vision of where you are headed – we are destined to take any path, with each step adding to the confusion and conflict of an uncertain future.

The complete difference in these two life approaches is that one exerts internal control over the extent of happiness to be realized along the way while the other must rely on external stimuli (a drug, an impulse purchase, a funny TV show) to bring fleeting moments of happiness. It's the difference between being happy on purpose, with a purpose, versus waiting for happiness to find you or having to create it superficially.

The Extremely Complex Link between Happiness and Decision-Making

For many of us, our immediate futures – tomorrow, next week and maybe even next month – seem pretty clear. But, over the longer time horizon it becomes more difficult to correlate the choices we make now with the future consequences of those choices. It's a disconnect that often leads to choosing instant gratification over a future reward largely because the abstract of time seems to allow it. There's always more time to do the right thing, right? I want to hit the snooze button on my alarm once, twice, maybe even three times because it brings me the instant gratification of additional, blissful sleep. With 24 hours in the day, what difference will additional half hour of sleep make?

These seemingly insignificant decisions can accumulate throughout the day – choosing a piping hot pastry over a healthy breakfast; spending four dollars on a Starbucks drink, skipping an afternoon workout, watching three hours of TV right before bedtime – all bringing fleeting moments of well-being without noticeable consequences. However, when one such day turns into two days, or a week, or a month, the fine line between what are wrong choices and what have become uncontrollable habits gradually dissolves and the consequences are compounded.

To put this in a familiar, real life perspective, consider the compounding effect of impulse purchases. When we toss our budget aside to buy the next great gadget, the justification is found in the amount of time we have to make up for the purchase – "I'll put aside additional savings next month." But, how do we know we won't be tempted next month by another shiny object? And, what if the next price tag requires several months' worth of additional savings to make up the financial difference?

Impulse purchases, though seemingly inconsequential in the moment, are typically not isolated occurrences; they tend to occur in patterns dictated by habitual behavior. One hundred dollars spent this month on a gadget isn't likely to bankrupt anyone; even a monthly habit of spending a few hundred dollars on goodies can be sustainable for most people earning a decent paycheck. But what is the future consequence of these short term decisions? Would you be shocked to learn that it could cost you tens of thousands of dollars when you need it the most – when you are no longer able or willing to earn a paycheck? That's called, retirement, which is often forced upon us; and it may seem as if it's far enough down the road that minor indiscretions couldn't possibly have an adverse impact. Think again.

Consider the effect of just $100 not saved today for retirement. If, instead of buying a new gadget with a useful life measured in just months, you invest that $100 in a mutual fund that earns an average of 8 percent over the next 25 years — compounded annually — it would grow to nearly $700. Not a big deal you say? Well, to begin with, had you bought the gadget, it would be long gone by then; and you would have lost any opportunity to earn that $600.

Now, consider the extra $100 a week you spend on things you can't account for – the daily lattes, restaurant and fast food meals, drinks with friends, brand-name clothes, silly, gas for trips to nowhere, etc. If, instead, you invested the $400 (about

$13 a day) in some mutual funds that earns an average 8 percent per year – compounded annually – it would grow to $366,000.

Here's the kicker: If you choose instant gratification over future rewards and wait, say, 10 years to start investing, you would have to invest nearly three times that amount, almost $1,100 a month in order to accumulate the same $366,000. Such is the cost of time wasted. So trying to use the amount of time you think you have as justification for waiting just increases your costs which can reduce your chances of success.

"But, I'll be earning more money in ten years, so I can afford the increased cost of retirement." If you haven't heard anyone actually say this, you know they're thinking it.

But, there is a fundamental problem with that strategy. When people receive a pay raise, the rational and responsible action to take would be to increase their savings by that amount or at least proportionately. However, for most people, especially those without a clear vision or plan for the future, the tendency is to simply apply the additional dollars to their life-style. That's because people who lack a purpose for the additional dollars they earn tend to fall prey to the "more is better" philosophy thinking that each incremental improvement in lifestyle will bring more happiness.

Of course, we know that not to be true. At best, happiness rooted in consumption is fleeting which only increases the "risk of more" Think back to a time when you were earning one third less income than you are now. Were you happy then? Most people would tend to say they were. For those who say they weren't, the chances are, if they weren't happy then, they aren't happy now. But, for the rest of us, more money and spending didn't necessarily improve our happiness; it only produced more situations of happiness.

If the ability to increase our consumption was truly a source of genuine, sustainable happiness, how do we explain the disturbing fact that, according to the Center for Disease Control, the suicide rate for Americans, age 45 to 64, has increased by more 30 percent over the last decade?* Among white, middle-aged men – supposedly the highest-earning and wealthiest (relatively speaking) segment of our population, the rate has jumped by more than 50 percent. What choices do these people make along the way that leads to the ultimate choice of suicide; and what guided their decisions?

Their decisions couldn't have been based on a life purpose otherwise, they would have chosen life.

False Happiness can be Hazardous to Your Health

When you consider all of the leading causes of death – self harm, heart disease, road injuries, aids, cirrhosis, murder, stroke, drug abuse, lung cancer, and alcohol abuse – decisions and choices were made along the way that led to a diseased heart, or wreck less speeding on the highway, or that one last pill too many. How many of these people left behind situations of happiness – a family, a dream house, lots of friends, etc. – that couldn't bring them genuine, sustainable happiness?

Nobody sets as their life's purpose to destroy their lives or the lives of people they love; so, the only conclusion that can be drawn is that they "live with no purpose". Their decisions along the way were guided by impulse, instant gratification, or the need to numb (or end) the pain of emptiness. To be sure, you can count among those who choose to take their own lives or wreck them gradually over time, people confronted by an unexpected, catastrophic, life-changing event, who lacked the mechanisms for coping. But, how many of them began their painful journey with decisions as small, and insignificant as hitting the snooze button three or four time each day because they had no purpose that would propel them out of bed?

Thankfully, most people, regardless of whether or not they've discovered their life's purpose or have defined their goals, are not prone to such extreme behavior. There still exists in most of us a moral compass that, even amidst the chaos and confusion of indecision or bad decisions, steers us away from that which can cause us or others the most harm. But, lacking a clear purpose in life, it can't always steer us in a direction that can do the most good for ourselves and others – and that's what, ultimately, brings each of us the happiness and fulfillment we desire.

Happiness Doesn't Come Easily

Unless you've won the lottery of life and are naturally predisposed to happiness regardless of what life throws at you, which is rare, you will eventually come to realize that happiness is a choice. Of course, choosing happiness doesn't simply make it so. If our lives, and ultimately, our happiness, are the sum total of all of the choices we make, the very first, significant choice must be to discover our own path to happiness and then make the decisions, large and small, that will keep us moving forward.

When you are on your path to happiness, suddenly risks are worth taking, hard choices are worth making, and the prospect of mistakes or failure is alluring, not frightening, because, with each one, you know you will be propelled further down your path. With each milestone you reach, your outlook grows even more positive and the power of external forces working to derail you is diminished. With each day, whether you achieved success or not, you can tell yourself you did your very best with no regrets. And, with each additional minute you spend on your path to happiness, your appreciation for what you have grows, ruling out any sense of wanting.

Is it as blissful as I'm making it sound? Not at all; it's actually a lot of hard work. You're not just changing your appearance, which might only require a diet or a makeover; you are changing your state-of-mind, which requires the rewiring of the most complex computer on the face of the earth – your brain.

It's your brain that controls your traits, your habits and the thousands of minute decisions you make every day. But your brain, which only wants to do what you think you want, is in a constant struggle with a more powerful human force – your emotions, your feelings. And, in the end, feelings and emotions almost always trump rational thought. More often than not, your brain caves to your emotions and acts accordingly; except when the brain is trained to control them as well. However, absent discipline and the proper state-of-mind, training the brain to overcome emotions is a steep uphill climb.

Finding and staying on your path to happiness requires a Commitment to purpose, Discipline (the ability to follow your path regardless of what life gives you), and Contentment (appreciating what you have along the way) – three critical ingredients not typically found together in the human DNA. Commitment to purpose without discipline can still result in chaos, and, without contentment, there is always the "risk of more." Few people are wired with all three at once, and most people have yet to develop any of them.

Why this Book had to be written?

I've been fortunate enough to be able to follow my own path to happiness, pursuing my passion for helping others to become high achievers in all aspects of their lives. In my work with people of all backgrounds, I have found that the true high achievers – those who are ascending to the pinnacle of success in both their professional lives and personal lives – are the ones who can constantly convert their thoughts into decisions that lead to positive outcomes. Having the ability to do that, deliberately and effortlessly, enables them to stay focused on their purpose which is the key to forming decisions with clarity, confidence and conviction. Does this make them immune from making bad decisions? Not at all; however, their confidence is what allows them to absorb the risk of bad decisions while forging ahead until they get it right. With a clearly defined purpose as their compass, they know they will eventually get back on the right path.

What separates true high achievers from other "successful" people is how they measure success. High achievers don't measure their success in terms of their bank account or the size of their business; rather, their only benchmarks are the life accomplishments that keep them moving down their path to happiness.

I know from my work with my clients, that anyone can develop the necessary traits and the ability to master their decision-making so that it puts them in control in their pursuit of happiness. This book is a personal journal of my experiences working with high achievers, utilizing the concepts, practices and advice of people who have achieved success in all aspects of their lives – their finances, their relationships, their business and, most importantly, their inner selves.

Essentially, I wrote the book I've long searched for but could not find as recommended reading for anyone who wants to transform their life that doesn't contain psychological jargon or impractical, beneficial applications. In fact, within the pages of this book are several technology-based applications that can be downloaded to your smart phone and applied as simple, daily activities designed to coach you in the development of the critical habits and decision-making capabilities shared by high achievers.

The first section of the book takes you on your own personal journey to finding your path to happiness offered with practical applications for developing the traits and habits to keep you there. You'll discover that the potential for leading a happy life resides within you; but, more importantly, you'll uncover the tools that can unleash that potential.

The second section provides a detailed guide for simplifying your decision-making in all aspects of your life, which will clear your path of obstacles and wrong turns. Simplifying the decision-making process doesn't guarantee you'll always make the right decisions; however, it is the essential key to eliminating the chaos and confusion which can cloud your vision and put you off track. The chapters are full of simple, practical applications and exercises that, with each use, can multiply your happiness on a daily basis.

Above all else, *The Daily Happiness Multiplier* was written to remind you that the journey to happiness, while full of hard choices, hard work and even disappointment, should bring you immense enjoyment and the satisfaction of daily fulfillment along the way. That is the essence of happiness.

Why you should get the workshops for each of the systems outlined at the end of each chapter?

- **Discover in-depth coaching-planning-achieving™ on all the systems presented that is not mentioned anywhere in the book or available anywhere else.**
- **You get a re-usable worksheet with empowering questions to unearth the hidden answers inside of you.**
- **You get a sample filled worksheet that guides how to use the concept or tool and find the secrets that are hidden inside your head.**
- **You get a video that you can keep on watching for the rest of your life.**
- **Only $52 for each workshop and value that is 10 times more.**
- **Future plans for buyers to enroll in a subscription plan to receive updates to the system.**
- **Receive special offers towards our programs.**

- **Get the entire deck of cards(52 Cards-52 Systems) at** http://www.BizActionCoach.com/product/the-deck-of-cards-workshop-system/

Systems to implement as a habit
when applicable to your situation:

I. Define your Purpose with the following steps:
  1. Use the workshop to discover your hidden abilities that you are a genius at.
  2. Let the workshop uncover the ways to create value that is greater than what you believe.
  3. Write your mission statement that incorporates your uniqueness.

Make life meaningful with The Purpose Builder™ workshop at http://www.BizActionCoach.com/product/the-purpose-builder-workshop/

II. Make your inner core stronger to deal with everyday issues:
  1. Use the workshop to discover and organize your most important daily appointment and understand your core.
  2. Plan and implement one activity in each aspect of your core.
  3. Put it in motion at least one of it the same day and not wait for tomorrow.

Be a Rock with The Core You™ workshop at http://www.BizActionCoach.com/product/the-core-you/

III. Build a strong resilience System:
1. Identify areas in which you need to be resilient.
2. Make a list of strategies using help from the workshop. Implement the first one to three at least the same day.
3. Develop Actions that need to be taken in those situations to be very resilient.

Be prepared to face any difficulty with The Resilience Developer™ workshop at http://www.BizActionCoach.com/product/the-resilience-developer/

IV. Avoid The Daily Happiness Trap:
1. Identify top 5 associations you have for happiness that also bring you sadness and disappointment.
2. Identify what to detach from and what to attach to with help from the workshop below.
3. Build a list of activities to attach to true happiness.

Avoid false happiness with The Happiness Trap™ workshop at http://www.BizActionCoach.com/product/the-happiness-trap/

V. Enhance your own self on a daily basis:
1. Divide your goals into categories that will enhance you on a daily basis.
2. Develop strategies using help from the workshop and build list of actions.
3. Build accountability on a daily basis.

Better yourself every day with The Daily "Me" Enhancer™ online workshop at http://BizActionCoach.com/product/the-daily-me-enhancer/

VI. Build your vision:
1. Using the concepts explained in depth in the workshop build a comprehensive vision about every aspect of your life.
2. Write it out on a single statement that combines the how, the what, and the why.
3. Plan out how you will chase your vision on a daily basis.

Build the foundation for your success with The Vision Builder™ online workshop at http://BizActionCoach.com/pre-recorded-workshops/

VII. Create Value in what you do:
1. From the systems explained in the workshop, understand how value is created.
2. Write out the areas where you will create more value than what you currently offer and with the workshop discover the secret to price your products in a way where your products don't compete on price.
3. Plan out how the strategies and activities to offer that value.

Excel yourself with others with The Value Creator™ online workshop at http://BizActionCoach.com/product/the-value-creator/

Get the entire deck of cards (52 Cards-52 Systems) at
http://www.BizActionCoach.com/product/the-deck-of-cards-
workshop-system/

**Please complete the exercise on the next page before
proceeding to read the first chapter.**

What thought or thoughts come to your mind after reading this chapter?

_____

_____

_____

_____

_____

_____

_____

What decisions have you made about the thought or thoughts you had?

_____

_____

_____

_____

_____

_____

_____

What Growth Actions would you take today or by a specific date to implement your thoughts?

_____

_____

_____

_____

_____

_____

_____

A True Story

In 1994, I was working in San Diego, California in an export-import company. The company was a big company but I was getting paid nominal to the quality of work that I was delivering. I had also applied at five different universities and University of Florida was ready to accept me. At that time, I had no savings and had no idea of how I would pay for the Tuition. Forget the tuition; I didn't have the money to buy even a plane ticket. So I took a greyhound bus from California to Florida. I travelled in the greyhound bus for a total of three days. It was very difficult to travel in that bus for that long, but I was happily reading the college books I had gotten from India and the books and the sight- seeing kept me engaged and happy in the journey. This is the power of happiness along the journey of life.

Chapter 1

finding your
path to happiness

d o happy people make better decisions? While it may give the disagreeable among us one more reason to group chronically happy people, there is a growing body of scientific evidence that suggests happy people, while not necessarily smarter than unhappy people, may have enhanced mental capabilities that can boost their capacity to make better decisions.

The findings by various neurological studies of people with a sunny disposition indicate a greater capacity for concentration, recall, analysis, judgment, perception control and creativity, all of which can lead to quicker decisions made with more confidence.

That doesn't mean they never make bad decisions. No one is immune from mistakes. However, because happy people tend to be more optimistic, they are willing to accept their mistakes because they know they will eventually get to the right decision. Their faith in the future allows them to continuously move forward because, although they may not know exactly how things will turn out all right, they just know that they will eventually.

Studies also show that happy people are better able to analyze data and draw conclusions more quickly. Because they tend to know what they want, or what will feed their happiness state, they have a more established set of criteria and are able to dismiss choices that don't meet their standards. And because they tend to value life to a much greater degree than gloomy people, happy people are better able to quickly eliminate any choices that have the potential to do harm to them or their family's health and well-being.

Happy people are also better able to recognize and, therefore, avoid dealing with frivolous problems and, instead, focus on those that they have a reasonable expectation of solving. That equates to less frustration, less wasted time and greater productivity at work or in their personal lives. Along the same lines, happier people seem to have a greater capacity for concentration, allowing them to multi-task. Perhaps that explains why women are better than men at multi-tasking. Studies have shown that women tend to be the happier of the sexes.

What Makes People Happy?

So, if we are to believe the research, which even the scientists admit is flawed (after all, how can we truly measure happiness?), then the key to better decision-making at all levels would seem to lie in our state of happiness. But, it doesn't answer the more critical, billion dollar question of how we can find true happiness. At least half of the answer lies in our genetic make-up, and therefore is largely out of our control. The sunny or cloudy predisposition we are handed at birth becomes the default setting for our level of happiness. Some of us are inherently more inclined to find satisfaction in life while others are in a constant search for more.

Fortunately, a large portion of our happiness state, as much as 40 percent of it, is within our power to choose and control situations that increase our happiness level. Only in recent decades has there been any kind of interest in uncovering the "secret to attaining happiness." More recently, an entire academic community has emerged that focuses exclusively on the "science of happiness." This new scientific discipline, referred to in academic circles as "positive psychology," seeks to answer the question posed by billions of people throughout the world, "what can I do to be happy," and then provide the psychological mechanism to attaining a happy state.

The science is still relatively new, and while much of it is subject to ongoing guesswork, there is fairly broad consent on many aspects of the cause and effect of happiness in people. There is also wide agreement that our brain holds the key to turning a frown into a perpetual smile. We might be able to fool our brain into creating moments of good feelings; however, in order to achieve a true state of happiness or well-being, those of us with a less sunny disposition will actually have to rewire or retrain our brain in positive ways so it knows what makes us content. That takes work and a commitment to learning what makes you content.

First, you have to be able to define your happiness and recognize the difference between that which is only fleeting and that which is an enduring state of mind. You may have already started on your list of things that make you happy, which is great; however, before you can make the transformation to lifelong contentment, you need to be aware of some of the happiness traps that can divert you from your mission.

Finding Happiness In Spite of Money

A lot depends on how you define 'happiness', and the role that money plays in your life. For many people, their level of happiness is based on a comparison of their lifestyle to another's. If they can keep up with the Jones, then they think they are happy. To them status achievement is the measure of happiness. At the extreme end you will find people who spend money that they don't have, to buy things they don't really need, just to impress people they might not even like.

For others, happiness is defined more from the positive feelings they have about themselves which may have little to do with money. It's more about the level of trust, love, support and respect they receive from friends, family and colleagues. In fact, for these people, money can actually get in the way of the positive feelings they yearn for. At the extreme end of this group are the rare people who might even be willing to endure a life of poverty if it would generate more positive feelings.

The Color of Money

The difference between these two groups of people may lie in the way they perceive the role of money in their life. Certainly, for most people, money is a means to an end. That end for status seekers may be more status, which could mean that can never have enough money. Ben Franklin observed that, "The more a man has, the more he wants. Instead of filling a vacuum, it makes one." Ben may have been implying that these people may never be completely happy.

Other people use money to help them serve a purpose in life, and, while they like the fact that they have money to enjoy a particular lifestyle, they don't lose sight of the things that money can't buy. For them, money brings satisfaction, but their happiness comes from what they achieve in life.

The Risk of "More"

Most of us have been conditioned throughout our lives to strive ever-upward in pursuit of more. It's the sole objective of advertisers to make us believe that our lives will be better if we own their product. And, as is fairly typical in our western culture, many people tend to measure their own lifestyle based largely on a comparison with others rather than criteria rooted in personal beliefs and values. In the pursuit of more, people lose sight of what they have which is really the only proof of what they can reasonably expect to produce, both now and in the future. The failure to appreciate the lifestyle increases the "risk of more" with absolutely no guarantee of increased happiness.

What's the Color of Your Money?

Money in and of itself is not the root of evil; rather, it is the love of money that can misrepresent a person's sense of happiness. When placed in the proper perspective, money can be an enabler of happiness when it allows people to be themselves and keep their focus on the things that are most important in life. The key is to treat money the way it was intended, as a tool to achieve your goals and build a life that you envision. When money becomes the goal, or your life turns into a debt spiral, true happiness may become elusive.

For the sake of what?

If a life of true happiness is possible, it can only be achieved through the pursuit of a purpose draped in your beliefs and values – What is it you truly believe in? What is it you really care about? Without which your life may be simply defined by an endless "pursuit of more" and that can never bring fulfillment. When people don't have a purpose for the money they accumulate, the natural tendency is to surrender to the pursuit of more, assuming that an incremental upgrade in their lifestyle will somehow make them happier. Only after a soul-robbing number of years in doing this, do they realize that the happiness of consumption is short-lived and their lives are still void of any sense of overall well-being.

Try thinking about the time in your life when your income was half of what it is today. Were you happy then? Chances are you were. Did the increase in money and spending since that time improve your happiness, or did it just create certain situations for you to feel happy in the moment? Looking forward, what will you do with the next 50 percent increase in your income? Will it serve a purpose or will it be added to your life-style? The difference for most people is whether they have a values-centered vision for the future or a momentary desire for "more."

Which Comes First: Happiness or Success?

Have you ever found yourself musing inwardly about how happy you would be if only...? We've all done that: "I'll be happy when I finally get that raise;" or, "I'll be a lot happier when I no longer have any debt;" or any other circumstance in which you see the grass as greener if your situation were different.

Most of us have been conditioned from an early age that, if we work hard we will be successful, as if, somehow, that will make us happier. Yet, it always seems that, once we achieve a certain level of success, someone moves the goal posts, and there is a new level that must be achieved. Consider the young college student who sacrificed everything in order to get into a top medical school. When he did get accepted, he realized that any happiness would have to be delayed until he graduated. When he did finally land a position with a hospital, all he could think about was starting his own practice...and on it goes. If success, at least as it's defined by this doctor, leads to happiness, he may never find it.

How many people do you know who have great careers but are not happy? How many celebrities who have reached the pinnacle in their business have thrown their lives away – through drugs, alcohol or suicide? Is it possible that many of these people were happiest when they were forced to find meaning in their lives before success came to them? Could their unhappiness be the result of the pressures of success?

What if, instead, we reverse the equation? If first achieving success is not a guarantee of finding happiness, then is it more likely that first finding happiness could lead more easily to success? Is it possible that, by focusing on finding happiness right now, no matter your situation, success can become a natural extension of your happiness? Can a positive attitude and outlook on life produce better outcomes in relationships and business or educational endeavors? If we work at cultivating happiness when life is a struggle, then wouldn't we increase the opportunities for achieving our goals?

If we consider, for the moment, that all of that is true, then we could conclude that happiness is the true measure of success. And, when the power of happiness is used to make others happy, it becomes the ultimate expression of success.

Would You Recognize Happiness if it were Right in Front of You?

Everyone knows some happy people, the type that greets you with an authentic smile and an unconditional expression of graciousness. Their first words out of their mouth form either a compliment or a genuine query into you and your family's health or welfare. And, when asked about their family, they respond with gratitude, not just for being asked, but also for the chance to praise life. Even if they are experiencing difficulties, they will give you a "glass half full" perspective and focus on the good things that are happening in their life.

Habitually happy people have several distinct traits in common, some of which you may not see on the surface, but are in constant motion in their daily lives:

Focus on Relationships: They focus on their relationships with their family, friends and relatives. Quality is more important than quantity and opportunities for deep conversations are relished. Research has shown that people who engage in more substantive conversation rather than trivial small talk experienced greater satisfaction in their relationships.

First in Caring: An abundance of research supports the notion that, people who volunteer or, in some way, routinely care for others are happier in their lives. Clinical research has uncovered a "helpers high" in givers not unlike the overjoyed state experienced in a drug-induced high.

Healthy and Well: Runners also experience a "high" after reaching a certain stage in their run. This same sense of well-being can be felt by anyone who regularly exercises. We also know that general attention to health can produce better moods and mental well-being. Just the act of drinking eight glasses of water each day as prescribed by health and nutrition experts can generate positive feelings.

Great Flow: When you get on a roll with activity or project and become totally immersed to the point when you lose track of time, you are considered by psychologists to be in a state of "flow." It typically occurs for people who are working towards a meaningful, long-term goal and find the activities involved motivating, challenging or stimulating. This is typical of athletes trying to get to the next level, or musicians trying to master a challenging piece, or anyone who is intent on stepping up from their comfort level to learn a new skill. It has been found that people who regularly experience this state of flow develop other positive traits that enhance their overall well-being.

Spiritual Engagement and Community: On this, the research is virtually indisputable – people who engage in spiritual activities tend to be happier. Their research validated link between prayer or meditation and well-being due to its calming and stress-reducing effect. Studies also show that people who engage in meditative activities are better able to invoke positive feelings. People who believe in a higher being feel a stronger sense of purpose giving their lives more meaning, and when they become involved in religious activities, they tend to find comfort in the strong social support and sense of community. The social engagement is said to be the strongest link between religious or community involvement and happiness.

Emphasis on Unique Strengths: Experts in positive psychology have found that the happiest people are those that have discovered and incorporated their unique strengths in their daily lives. In his book, *Unique Ability: Creating the Life You Want, Life Coach Dan Sullivan* theorizes that each of us have this incredible force within us comprised of our personal talents, passions and skills, but that few of us have identified, much less utilized them.

When this superior ability is utilized it can energize us and the people around us because of the passion behind it. It's a skill or talent we want to perform as much as possible and constantly strive to improve because, when we do it, it brings maximum happiness in life. Your unique ability, that what you do best in life and what you love doing most, will give you purpose (a key pillar of happiness), especially if it can be used for the greater good of the community.

Eternally Optimistic and Resilient: We've all seen the studies that show the benefits of optimism. An optimistic outlook can reduce stress and increase our tolerance for pain and hard knocks. To optimists, failure is just a temporary setback – just another opportunity to pursue. Optimists are resilient and, as the Japanese proverb goes, "Fall seven times and stand up eight."

Do you share any of these traits? Can having just one or two be enough to make you a happy person? It's a step forward to becoming a "whole person". For instance, optimistic people tend to be healthier and are generally better at forging strong relationships. Based on the work of philosopher, Mortimer Alder, a "whole person" incorporates all seven of the key elements of daily living: family, health, education, career, service, financial, and spiritual. According to Alder, "Whole persons are engaged in a lifetime quest to achieve balance and agreement in all aspects of their lives and continually seeking to develop their full human potential." So, why stop at one or two traits. If you work to develop all of the traits that cultivate happiness, it is much more likely to be embodied state of being.

Developing the Traits of Happiness

According to Sonja Lyubomirsky, PhD, an expert in the science of happiness, "Research is showing pretty convincingly now that happiness is really within us, it's not outside of us. It's in what we do. It's sort of how we act, how we think every day of our lives." In her research, Lyubomirsky has found that people can force themselves to truly become happier, but because people can easily regress to their genetically-imposed happiness default settings, it can be an uphill climb for most. However, realizing that 40 percent of our happiness quotient is within our power, through the control of our daily thoughts and actions, people can, in fact change their own default-settings.

Of course, achieving a state of happiness by countering a genetic disposition is not an easy endeavor. In fact, it requires a work ethic not unlike developing a highly refined skill-set or sculpting your body into a lean and powerful machine. It's not quite as easy as telling yourself to be happy today, although that's a good start; you actually need to work at being happy. Many psychologists would argue that happiness is a habit that needs to be cultivated which includes training the brain to perceive life from a completely different perspective.

Recognizing the importance of attaining as state of happiness in making better decisions, I've worked with my clients on building happiness habits that can lead to development of the essential traits that will sustain it.

Chapter 2 is devoted to the challenge of building happiness habits and offers a process for meeting that challenge starting today.

Systems to implement as a habit when applicable to your situation:

I. Build The Daily Happiness Path™ with the following steps:
1. What are the top three decisions that you have made in the last week to 10 days that you know were wrong or you feel were a mistake?
2. From the workshop discover the hidden process of improvising your decision making skills. Or use The Decision Simplifier™ system to develop better decision making skills.
3. With the help of the workshop, arrive at what needs to be done by when and who will do it to put you on the path of daily happiness.

Build your own hidden happiness path with The Daily Happiness Path™ workshop at http://www.BizActionCoach.com/product/the-daily-happiness-path/

Or Download **Rajparth mobile application on Apple or Android**.

II. Eliminate More with The More Eliminator™:
1. With the concepts explained in the workshop, make a list of all the things you want more of in life.

2. Learn from the workshop how to eliminate those to get more of what you want.
3. With the tools described in the workshop, build a list of ideas and strategies that can create an everlasting value for others.
4. Work on at least one of those today.

Get More in life with The More Eliminator™ workshop at   http://www.BizActionCoach.com/product/the-more-eliminator/

III. Build your Not-to-do-List:
1. Identify and make a list of activities and material things that haven't brought much improvement in your own inner-self.
2. With the help of the workshop, make a not-to-do list of activities resulting from decisions you make.
3. Implement one to three of the activities in the next 24 hours.

Manage your time effectively with The Not-to-Do List Builder™ workshop at http://BizActionCoach.com/product/the-not-to-do-list-builder/

IV. The Micro-Decision Simplifier™ System:
1. Make a list of top 3-5 impulse purchases you had made over the last week to 10 days that you were very unhappy with.

2. With the help from the workshop discover the causes of decisions to not work in your favor and apply the hidden truths to make more right decisions.

3. With the tools explained in the workshop, build the list of activities you will do to change your micro-decision making habits.

Make your daily decisions more productive with The Micro-Decision Simplifier™ workshop.

V. Building a Stronger Character System:

1. Make a list of top one to three daily activities you do or will do that show your commitment to your purpose.

2. From the workshop, connect the activities for your purpose that improves your daily character.

3. Make a list of top one to three daily activities you do or will do that shows daily improvement discipline in your life.

Get closer to a great destiny with The Character DNA™ online workshop at http://BizActionCoach.com/product/the-character-dna/

Get the entire deck of cards (52 Cards-52 Systems) at http://www.BizActionCoach.com/product/the-deck-of-cards-workshop-system/

Chapter 1: Workbook Assignment

- Understand that happiness is a choice and make a deliberate one to find your path to happiness today. Schedule an hour to reflect on the decisions you are making in your life right now and place them in the context of your values, beliefs, and purpose.

- Be able to clearly articulate your own values and beliefs. What beliefs and attitudes do you hold regarding family, health, security and service to others? Then prioritize them. If you had to trade off one for another, which would it be?

- Create your vision for a good life – today and for the rest of your life. What exactly does it entail – for you, your family and your community? What unique ability or passion do you want to make as the cornerstone of your life? What would you want to be able to say about yourself? What would you want other people to say about you?

- Identify opportunities in your daily life – at work, at home, in your community – that will keep you moving down the path to your vision. Explore how you will use that focus to minimize the setbacks and keep you moving forward. Will you learn from them or will you let them divert you from your vision?

Be deliberately optimistic today. If your tendency is to see the glass as half full, use a setback to exercise your optimism by purposefully viewing it as a temporary occurrence and then take credit for positive occurrences.

Please complete the exercise on the next page before proceeding to read the next chapter.

What thought or thoughts come to your mind after reading this chapter?

_____

_____

_____

_____

_____

_____

_____

What Decision or Decisions have you made about the thought or thoughts you had?

_____

_____

_____

_____

_____

_____

_____

What Growth Actions would you take today or by a specific date to implement your thoughts?

_____

_____

_____

_____

_____

_____

_____

A True Story

When I had taken the greyhound bus, I had also packed everything in a big brown box as I didn't have the freedom to spend money on buying another suitcase. When I reached Gainesville greyhound bus station, I had to take a taxi cab from the station from University of Florida campus and the cab driver said he could only drop me to the curb of the road that took me to the dorm. At that time I had to walk almost a football field with all my luggage and carry that big brown box with me. The student crowd over there stared at me and I had all the reasons to feel embarrassed and unhappy, but I didn't. I was determined to make it to the end zone and when I did two students standing near the dorm door clapped. That just multiplied the amount of happiness I had at the moment.

Chapter 2

habits to happiness

t's reasonable to accept the academic doctrine that happiness is a result of having certain character traits such as self-esteem, optimism, extroversion, etc. These along with all of our traits are elements of our personality that, once established, remain relatively stable throughout our lives and are at the core of all of our thoughts, beliefs, emotions and behaviors. It's reasonable to assume that, if we are handed these traits at birth and they're nurtured in us while we are young, they will carry us through our lifetimes. If we are born a happy person then we will probably die a happy person.

If, however, we are all created equal by God, all instilled with the traits He designed for us, aren't we all born happy?

If, as Dr. Lyubomirsky's research shows, happiness resides within us, then it can be construed that we are, indeed, born happy. It is from that point forward, however, when external factors begin to shape the way we utilize our God-given traits, and, exposure to external elements can mutate our traits and even create new, undesirable traits. A baby born into an environment of poverty, abuse and discouragement has little chance to exercise his or her positive traits; and, as long as he remains in that environment, he or she is all the more likely to develop negative traits that will perpetuate a state of unhappiness.

Unfortunately, it's not much easier for children born into privilege who may be exposed to an environment in which happiness is falsely pursued through the promise of "more." Parents who have yet to discover their true source of happiness, will often pursue it materially, which can never bring true fulfillment or contentment; thus, they continually crave more. This character trait is then infused into the child who then equates happiness with having more stuff.

When material pursuits are substituted for the pursuit of self-discovery and personal fulfillment, happiness will always be fleeting, and the persona of happiness we reflect to the rest of world is nothing more than a mask. Underneath that mask lives a child or an adult, who doesn't know true happiness. It's not surprising then, when we hear of the tragic death by suicide or drug overdose of successful, wealthy celebrities; even more tragic, are the high rate of depression and the increasing rate of drug abuse and suicide among young people across the entire economic strata.

For those of us who were handed a more sour temperament, happiness becomes a conscious choice. Aside from putting on a mask every now and then, absolute happiness is largely elusive for people who are predisposed to pessimism, compulsiveness or other negative character traits. For those who genuinely want to transform their temperament, well-meaning advice is to "be more positive" or "be more outgoing."

You Can Change it if you want

The good news is that our personalities are not encoded into us like our hair color. The predispositions we are handed at birth can be influenced by the world around us as well as our own efforts. We do, in fact, have the power to influence our own destinies. The things we do in our daily lives ultimately shape our future. While it's true that our character traits affect our behavior, psychologists have proven that our traits can be shaped by our behavior. When done consciously, or deliberately, there is nothing that can stop us from transforming ourselves in a positive way.

One way to get on the path to happiness is to simply start acting happy. You may not feel like it, or it may be very uncomfortable, but even pretending to be optimistic or acting like your outgoing can have a "saying-is-believing" effect that could eventually take hold. We all "faked" a new role in life that required new behaviors and attitudes (i.e., becoming a new parent) until the role grew on us as if it were perfectly natural. Of course, being in a situation that requires that transformation, such as raising a baby, provides much more motivation than simply saying you want to change.

Alternatively, we can look to changing or building character traits as a process fully equipped with a goal, a plan and specific action steps. Changing or building a trait requires retraining the brain to believe that it is a part of your being so that your behavior responds instinctively. It's much like creating a habit – after performing the new behavior consistently over a period of time, it becomes instinctive, automatic. In fact, one could think of habits as the building blocks of traits.

To become optimistic may require building several different habits that will reinforce the trait and make it endure over time.

Change is Possible for Addicts-How I Quit Smoking

Out of all the changes you make and you want to make, addiction is the hardest and most difficult change of all. Only a person who has made that change knows that and feels that. I have and I want to share how I did it. Because of a very troubled childhood and deserted teenage years, I had become a chain smoker when I was 19 years old. I had even tried to lock myself up in a bathroom, held a bottle of rat poison in my hand, and tried to kill myself. As luck would have it, I couldn't open the bottle being the skinny teen I was, I survived.

Three days after that incident, I was at the terrace of my apartment building in Mumbai, alone and smoking. I was standing on the edge of the terrace holding the cigarette in my hand and it fell from my hands. I saw it falling down from the top of the apartment building and it wasn't the cigarette I saw, I saw myself. It wasn't the ashes that splattered all over, it was my brain. That was a scary sight. At that point I asked God, is that what will happen to me? At that point I sneezed twice and instead of mucus I had black mucus and layers of black stuff come out of my nose. At that time, I held a superstitious belief that if I sneezed twice, whatever I wished or thought before will come true. That was the day I gave up smoking and decided to take charge of my life and fight it through.

That's how I quit smoking. That's when I realized you have to develop good habits that make you live and be happy.

Habits to Happiness

We've all had experience with building new habits or breaking old ones. I think we would all agree that it's hard; so much so that many of us don't attempt it very often, except perhaps when forced to change a behavior for health reasons, or for love of others. In the case of building "happiness" habits, it very well could come down to both of those reasons. The desire to live a healthier, longer and more fulfilling life, or to improve your relationships at home or work, can be strong motivating factors for committing to new habits. For many people, it's simply a desire to choose happiness over sadness.

Regardless of the motivation, it's important to distill it down to a clearly defined goal which should be developing a particular trait or series of traits that can change your disposition – to be optimistic; to be outgoing; to utilize my strength; to forge strong relationships, etc. to become a whole person.

Next, you need to identify the activities or behaviors associated with those traits that you can naturally incorporate into your daily life. For instance, using the traits described in Chapter 2, you can identify specific behaviors or activities you could perform each day that, when formed as a habit, will contribute to developing that particular trait. It might look something like this:

Strong relationships – finding ways to make your relationships the center of your life

- A family that eats, prays and plays together stays together: Establish one new family gathering opportunity every three months, i.e., – Sunday night dinners together, game night, attending church, volunteering, a monthly Saturday outing, etc. Allow each new opportunity time to take hold before introducing another one.
- Schedule date nights with your spouse. While dining and entertainment make for nice dates, it's the quality time together that counts.
- Capture moments of happiness each day – a hug from your child, a spontaneous family gathering, the comfort of a friend, recognition of your efforts – and make those the thoughts you take to bed.
- Schedule a weekly call to a friend, parent, or sibling (no Facebook or email). Go short on small talk and long on a deep conversation about your relationship – what makes it special; what you would like to do to strengthen it; find ways to learn new things about the person, etc.

Caring for others – finding ways to make a difference

- Schedule a time each week to make contact with an elder or someone in need.

- Volunteer with a community group that cares for the elderly or people in need.
- Replace a common purchase you make with a gift to someone else – try for once in two weeks.

Focus on health and wellness – finding ways to build a strong mind and body

- The big one: If you're not already, schedule at least 20 minutes of exercise each day. The best time is the morning – it's easier to schedule and it will boost your energy all day.
- Set a goal for losing weight or achieving a level of performance in your workouts or a sport and create a plan of daily activities to meet the goal within 3 months. Map your activities and record your daily results.
- Get a minimum of 7 hours sleep and wake up the same time each day. We all know the benefits – better health, more energy, positive attitude, etc. Make it ritual, especially on workdays. Eliminate all of the things that might prevent you from getting a full night's sleep such as, disconnecting your eyes from glaring screens at least an hour before you want to fall asleep. If you read from an actual book instead of a tablet or computer you can read right up to the time you fall asleep.
- Drink eight glasses of water each day. There's no denying the health benefits of keeping your body hydrated. Find a way. Make a habit of drinking a tall glass of water before breakfast, lunch and dinner – that's three. Keep a water

jug and glass at your desk. Use flavor packets in your bottled water. Have some carbonated water after dinner.

- Nix the late morning or afternoon coffee and go for a walk instead – it provides the same effect (more energy) with more health benefits.

Getting in the "State of Flow" – finding ways to let your passion dominate your life

- There's one single habit that can unleash everything you need to get into a state of flow: Try to do your absolute best at all times; and when you think it can be better, repeat these six powerful words: "Up to now I have done this (the method, level of effort, or activity performed); From now on I will do this (how you would improve the method, level of effort or activity)."

- Identify your single greatest strength of which you are passionate (i.e. communication, interpersonal relations, motivating people, analysis, problem-solving, critical thinking, etc.) and find a new way to utilize it each day, at work, in your community, and at home for the benefit of others. Your goal should be to fill your day using nothing but your unique strength.

- Take five minutes first thing in the morning to plan your day and prioritize the essentials of the day. In addition to your work related activities, be sure to schedule and prioritize essential activities such as a volunteer activity, a call to a relative, date nights, family time, etc.

Spiritual engagement and community – finding ways to develop your positive attitude

- The big one: Schedule 15 to 30 minutes each day for prayer or meditation. Make it "sacred time" in which you unplug from everything – it's a can't-miss positive attitude generator.
- If you belong to a church, temple, any religious place or a community group in your town, join one of its social groups; volunteer. Make it a weekly activity.

Eternally optimistic and resilient – finding ways to know that things will always get better

- Surround yourself with optimistic people. Optimism is contagious, just as pessimism is. Avoid downers and hang positive, happy people.
- Reframe negative thoughts. When dark clouds appear, think of the sun that shines above them. Dark clouds come and go, but the sun will always be there. When something doesn't go right or bad things happen, dismiss is as a temporary occurrence and think about what will go right the next time.
- Take control. Bad luck or silly mistakes might play some part when things go wrong, but that doesn't excuse your misfortune. Take responsibility for your part and endeavor to make it right.
- End your day with gratitude. Keep a journal next to your bed and write down at least one great thing that happened and take inventory of the good things in your life. In other words, count your blessings. Equally

important, learn to express gratitude for the bad things that happen, because they are what optimists use to gain wisdom.

- Be a positive thinker. Make a point to find the silver lining in everything and think beyond the negative to the positive that will come of it.

How to Build Happiness Habits

The next step is to master the skill of building the habits that will lock in those behaviors or activities. We've all heard some variation of how to build a habit which typically includes a prescribed timeframe that must be exhausted in order for the habit to take hold. I've always ascribed to the Power of 21 in which, if you do anything for 21 consecutive days it becomes ingrained as a habit. Longer timeframes have been prescribed – 28 days or even 100 days – however, it's not so much the length of the habit-building cycle, it's your level of commitment and how you utilize the time that will determine the outcome.

Before starting, it's critical to map out a plan for successfully forming your new habits. You need vision, a goal and a deliberate plan for achieving it, otherwise it will have the same chance of success as some guilt-induced New Year's resolution, which, according to studies, fails more than 70 percent of the time. You're aiming for transforming your temperament, not losing a few pounds. Here is a proven process for converting a desired habit into a strategic plan for success:

Step 1: Discover Your Deeper Purpose

You may recognize the need to change – to develop a more positive outlook; to lose some weight; to be a better person, etc. But, without discovering the deeper purpose for changing, your efforts may be fleeting and, even if you are successful, you may never feel a sense of fulfillment, which is critical to achieving a state of happiness.

For the change you want, ask yourself, "Why?" What will be different in your life, and how will it create a greater good for you and those around you?

Your deeper purpose is not only the motivation you need, it becomes the beacon to guide all of your decisions along the way.

Step 2: Define the Elements of Truth

One of the primary reasons why people have difficulty with change is they tend to avoid the discomfort of self-discovery that must precede the change. If we can't honestly examine and accept our faults, we may never overcome the psychological or emotional inertia that is the challenge of change. If, for example, your desire is to lose 20 pounds, it would be important to accept the truth of why you are 20 pounds overweight. For instance,

- I eat too much junk food
- I love sugar
- I hate to exercise; I'm basically lazy
- I watch too much TV or spend too much time surfing the Internet
- I stay up too late and sleep too late

Yes, the truth does hurt, but it will free you to concentrate on the outcome you desire. And, unless you still live with your Mom, you're not likely to hear the truth from anyone but yourself.

Step 3: Visualize the outcome

What is the trait you are trying to acquire? To be more outgoing, or more caring of others! Whichever particular trait you are targeting, gain a clear understanding of how it will change your life. Envision yourself with that new trait and what it will mean in your daily interactions, your social life, and your career, and how that makes you feel. Make it real or you won't have the motivation needed to follow through.

Step 4: Realize the benefits

Write down the specific benefits you expect to derive from the new trait.

For example, being optimistic could bring the following benefits:

- Never fearing failure
- Controlling my own destiny
- See problems as opportunities
- Being more productive
- Creating a more positive environment
- Better, more positive relationships

Step 5: Choose the activity or behavior to perform

For any trait you want to form or strengthen, there may be several different activities or behaviors you can introduce into your daily life. Until you get in the habit of successfully forming new habits, it's best to focus on just one or two at a time. And, so that you are able to strike a healthy life balance in your new activities, it's recommended that you align them with both your personal and professional lives. You might choose a particular activity that contributes to your personal development and a separate activity to work towards a professional goal. Or, you can select one activity that can help you with both.

Finally, you should consider choosing an activity that keeps you focused on achieving a meaningful long-term outcome – a life milestone that may take a longer time to develop or nourish a trait. For example, preparing to successfully launch your children into college and adulthood would be considered a major life milestone that may require the development of several traits, both in you and your children. There may be a series of behaviors and activities that need to take hold over a long period of time that will instill the right habits – for you in your parenting role, and for your kids in their personal growth. A focus on certain traits such as strong relationships, caring for others, and resilience can provide the foundation for a successful transition.

Other life milestones might include retirement, starting a business, or starting a family, all of which are longer term goals which require as much emotional and psychological preparation as it does financial preparation. What's the nearest life milestone on your horizon, and what traits will help you achieve it in a positive way? What behaviors or activities will contribute to strengthening those traits?

What's Your Pringle?

We've all opened a can of Pringles haven't we? If you have, you're familiar with the sensation of peeling off the seal and having the aroma of fresh potato chips. You can't wait to taste that first, perfectly formed chip. The scent and the flavor of the neatly stacked chips become increasingly irresistible with each one you devour. Pretty soon half the stack is gone. Lee Brower, author of The Brower Quadrant, introduced this concept.

What if your passion was like opening a can of Pringles? What if, when you discover it, you can't stop thinking about it or finding ways to enjoy it? It's what gets you up in the morning, energizes you and empowers you to be the best you can be for the rest of the day. It may be a unique ability you discover, or, it could simply be one of those things you never seem to find time for, like reading a book, making a life journal, taking up a craft, taking long bike rides, or joining a yoga class – things you've spent a lot of time thinking about, but you never got around to because there was always something more pressing in your life. You know that these activities could bring you immense joy, but, for some reason, or excuse, you have managed to avoid doing it.

The biggest step you can take on your path to happiness is to open your can of Pringles each day and commit the time to do the things you've been depriving yourself of. You don't need anyone or anything else to get it done, just your own approval that it's OK to enjoy it.

Take a moment right now to make a list of your Pringles and commit yourself to indulging one time a day (or one time a week to start if you need more to time to rearrange other priorities).

What's My Daily Pringle?	✓	Time to Devote to it

Once you've identified two or three of your Pringles, create a weekly plan to make sure you can enjoy them. Determine how many hours at the outset you want to spend in the activities each day or week and then block the time. It may require that you start your day an hour earlier, or build a break into your work day. Of course, weekends are the ideal time to become immersed in your passion, but it shouldn't detract from family time unless it involves your family. Block the time – on your calendar, on your mobile daily planner, and in your mind, and don't let anything interfere with your schedule. After three or four weeks of pursuing your Pringle, you'll find that even wild horses couldn't drag you away from it.

Plan, monitor and measure
For each activity, establish a goal. For example:

> *I want to be 25 pounds lighter and in the*
> *best shape of my life within two years*

Your action plan may not consist of anything more than scheduling the time – making sure to actually block the time so that nothing else interferes. For this particular goal, your planned activities may require resources, such as a gym membership, exercise equipment, or a new food pantry. It's important to budget for your activities, which may be a separate habit to develop by itself.

For each long-term goal you will need to break it down into shorter benchmarks or milestones so you can more easily measure your progress. That's fairly easy to do when you have identified your planned activities. For this particular goal you may have the following as your planned activities:

- Drink 8 glasses of water each day
- Eat five helpings of fruit and vegetables each day
- Walk 2 miles per day
- Do 30 pushups and 50 crunches each day

These activities are easily tracked and measured. You either did them or you didn't. When combined with weekly or monthly benchmarks towards your goal, you will be able to see how your activities are working and stay motivated to keep on track. The most important element of tracking your progress is to make a journal of how you feel as you move towards your goal:

How's my energy level today?
How are my clothes fitting – are they getting looser?
How is my attitude today – more positive?
How does getting healthier make me feel?
How do I feel about the decisions I'm making?

Asking yourself how you feel about your activities or performance will reinforce your efforts because you will be constantly reminded of why you are doing it.

Turning Behavior or Activities into Habit

Initially, your key measurement is whether you are actually performing the activity as planned in order to form it as a habit. We developed a simple, but effective tool for our clients to use, called, The H3™ – Habits to Happiness Helper. They can use it as a desktop or bedside journal, or add it to their digital calendars on their computer, tablet or smart phone.

We recommend that you take the minute or two each day to handwrite your entrees. What we do know is that writing with your hand creates a more vivid physical memory or file in your brain so that it remains at the top of your mind, rather than buried deep in a heap of neurons. And, that can be very powerful in forming new habits.

Walk the Walk

Only you can hold yourself accountable for doing the things necessary to build a habit that will help you achieve your goals. Sure it helps to have a coach, or someone with whom you share your goals to reinforce that accountability or remind you to stay on track, but you are still the one who has to exercise your free will each day to make the right choices. You can desire change, set goals, plan your strategy, and enlist anyone you need to help, but it is not until you actually "walk the walk" that change occurs.

Perhaps the best way to walk the walk is to demonstrate to others your commitment and newly found passion by encouraging them to join you. When you are able to encourage others, you will sharpen your own awareness of the character trait you are trying to develop in yourself while reinforcing your decision to change. Many of the character traits people seek to form or strengthen are, in and of themselves, infectious. Optimism, enthusiasm, positive thinking, and other qualities get noticed and attract others who may want to change their outlook on life.

The Happiness Multiplier™ Mobile Application

The Happiness Multiplier™ Mobile Application is designed to do just that – multiply your happiness on a daily basis. Building the habits that lead to happiness requires that you focus on those aspects of your life that promote personal and professional growth, which is easier said than done. Most people have difficulty formulating the positive thoughts and pursuing those actions that keep them a growth mode, which is why many successful executives, athletes, and celebrities hire a life coach – to keep them on track. For the rest of us, who might not be able to afford that luxury, the Happiness Multiplier™ App becomes a personal coach that listens to you and then helps you to keep moving towards your growth objectives.

Like an effective life coach, it asks you the penetrating questions that require a moment of self-discovery while you pause and think through your next decision or action. The answers are not always clear, but, at least, you are forced to consider them in light of your happiness objective.

When used consistently throughout the day – it takes just 30 seconds to complete the application – its impact can be exponential in expanding your capacity to reap greater fulfillment on a daily basis. The Happiness Multiplier™ App is your 30-second personal coach that will keep you moving forward to pursue your personal and professional growth objectives, and it's available at any time and on an unlimited basis.

Chapter Workbook:

- Complete the workbook exercise in Chapter 2 if you haven't already (Clearly articulating your values)
- Identify the key trait (s) you want to strengthen
- Map out a plan for achieving a long-term goal linked to developing that trait
  - Clearly define your goal
  - Envision the outcome (how will it make you feel)
  - List specific benefits you will realize
  - Identify the specific activities you want to incorporate in your daily life
  - Monitor and measure your progress – keep a journal of your observations
- Download the Rajparth Mobile Application and begin using it today

Systems to implement as a habit
when applicable to your situation:

I. Strengthening your family relationship:
  1. With help from the workshop, discover the hidden systems that help you overcome challenges that prevent you from spending quality time with your family.
  2. Dedicate one meal (breakfast, lunch or dinner) a day to eat together as a family. If you can't do it every day,

do at least 5 days a week. What meal would you eat together as a family on what days of the week?

3. Dedicate a play time once or twice a week, when the entire family plays together. What days will you and your family play together?

4. Dedicate time to go to your church or temple or your holy place and pray together. What day of the week you would commit to do this?

Discover how you can make time to improve family relationships with The Family Relationship Builder™ workshop at http://www.BizActionCoach.com/product/the-family-relationship-builder/

II. Strengthening your spousal relationship:

1. With help from the workshop, discover and build daily systems and hidden strategies to make quality time you need to spend with your spouse.

2. What days can you commit to have dedicated date nights once a week or at least once a month?(For example: First Wednesday of every month or every Tuesday)

3. What day and time you can commit to have a weekly meeting with your spouse to discuss and plan the week ahead?

4. Can you find opportunities daily to commit to helping in your spouse's tasks by asking what can I do for you or how can I help you?

Discover how you can make time to improve spousal relationship with The Spousal Relationship Builder™ workshop at http://www.BizActionCoach.com/product/the-spousal-relationship-builder/

III. For People who have never exercised and want to begin exercising:
1. With help from the workshop, overcome the challenges that are preventing you from beginning to exercise.
2. Build your beginners routine with secrets explained in the workshop on how I did it myself when I had never exercised and weighed 230 lbs and now I weigh 165 lbs.
3. Continue the routine build for 21 consecutive days or 21 times in 5 weeks.

Overcome the hurdle of beginning to exercise with The Exercise Beginner™ workshop at http://BizActionCoach.com/product/the-exercise-beginner/

IV. Discovering the elements of Truth:
1. With help from the workshop discover the hidden elements of truth about yourself.
2. From the workshop discover the activities you need to develop on a daily basis to reach your true self that you want to be.
3. From the workshop learn the secrets of developing your customized discipline list to reach your true self.

Apply the immensity of the truth for achieving your goals with The Elements of Truth™ workshop at http://www.BizActionCoach.com/product/the-elements-of-truth/

V. The Ongoing personal and professional development system:

1. With the workshop discover the goals you need to have to improve yourself.
2. Learn the secret of successful implementation and build a system of strategic alternates.
3. Develop and execute activities on the secret components that help you develop personally and professionally every day.

Achieve your daily goals with The Personal and Professional Development System™ at http://www.BizActionCoach.com/product/the-personal-professional-development-system/

Get the entire deck of cards (52 Cards-52 Systems) at http://www.BizActionCoach.com/product/the-deck-of-cards-workshop-system/

Please complete the exercise on the next page before proceeding to read the first chapter.

What thought or thoughts come to your mind after reading this chapter?

_____

_____

_____

_____

_____

_____

_____

What Decision or Decisions have you made about the thought or thoughts you had?

_____

_____

_____

_____

_____

_____

_____

What Growth Actions would you take today or by a specific date to implement your thoughts?

_____

_____

_____

_____

_____

_____

_____

A True Story

When I was in college, I had to pay my own out-of-state non-resident tuition to University of Florida that was in excess of $25,000 a year. I had no money and I worked 4-5 jobs and took as many credits as I could to pay for the tuition and graduate successfully in flying colors. This was all possible because of my daily habits of waking up early no matter what time I slept, working hard to pay tuition through jobs, scholarships, grants, and some financial aid. I had a night shift in the library and I would say I really slept on the job! It was my daily drive and commitment and habits that got me through college on my own and fund my own tuition. Your daily habits early on in your career can take you a long way and if you feel you're late because you're old, you are never too late to start planning for a quantum leap in your life.

Chapter 3

why you should decide to decide more often

t's all too familiar to each of us – no matter how "gentle" the sound of our alarm, it's always a shrill reminder that our deep slumber is only temporary and we must face the day ahead. At that very instant, a choice is made – to hit the snooze button to allow for another ten minutes of blissful sleep; or press the off button and charge forward without hesitation. No matter which choice we make, a decision is behind it. Granted, it's a seemingly small decision, made in a semi-conscious state; but it will still have consequences.

That decision to sleep ten or twenty minutes later in the day can trigger a cascade of additional decisions that will very likely shape the outcome of your day. Consider this fairly typical day-in-a-life:

Having decided to press the snooze button twice, you are now twenty minutes behind your typical schedule. Instead of the healthy breakfast you try to eat each morning, you decide to grab a piece of toast with jam on the run. Instead of arriving ten minutes early for work, which usually allows you to get organized and charged, you arrive right on time but are forced to jump right in just to get on pace.

Your fast but unhealthy breakfast leaves you feeling empty, so you compensate by eating more than you typically do for lunch causing you to skip your 20 minute workout on the treadmill. Within an hour you start to feel sluggish making it very difficult to keep up your normal pace. Despite your rule of "no caffeine after lunch," you decide to down a cup of coffee prior to your late afternoon meeting with the management team but it can't clear the fog enveloping your thoughts.

Realizing it hasn't been one of your better days, and having skipped your lunchtime exercise, you decide to go to the gym after work hoping it can reenergize your mind and body. Of course it does, and between your racing metabolism and the remnants of caffeine in your blood, you can't get to sleep, so you decide to watch some Jerry Seinfeld reruns, almost ensuring a repeat of this morning's decision to hit the snooze button. And, because you know your clock gives you three snooze opportunities, you're likely to have a worse day tomorrow.

No big deal you say? We all have days like that, don't we? True enough, however, if you string enough days like that together, the hundreds or thousands of "small decisions" we make each day can have life-changing consequences. It's these "micro-decisions" we make constantly throughout the day that chain themselves together like a growing virus to form the habits – good and bad – that shape our daily lives, and, ultimately, our future.

The consequences are only compounded for married couples who engage in a battle of the snooze buttons each morning, especially when one spouse is asked to "cover" for the other, as in, "Honey, can you wake me up in ten minutes?" First, there is the threat of resentment that might build for the spouse who must take responsibility for both getting up on time. Then there is the catastrophic risk of neither getting up on time. The ensuing chaos, anger and frustration, especially if this is a daily habit, not only set an unfriendly tone for the day, it can lead to a compounding resentment that plays out in many other aspects of the relationship. It is, simply, not worth it. As the first major co-decision of the day – to hit or not to hit the snooze button – it can have a life changing, ripple effect on the relationship.

The Underestimated Power of Small Decisions

Many of the decisions we make each day are innocuous and inconsequential; however, on average, we also make around 7 to 15 decisions of consequence, whether it's to accept an invitation to a party, spend an extra $5 on a latte, skip a workout, or to switch funds to another mutual fund. Of course some are more consequential than others, but then consider that even the small decisions add up and compound over time. The twice-weekly latte, for instance, can amount to thousands of dollars over the course of your lifetime.

> *"We must not, in trying to think about how we can make a big difference, ignore the small daily differences we can make which, over time, add up to big differences that we often cannot foresee."*
> —**Marian Wright Edelman**, Activist

We are more likely to be aware of the "big decisions" or more conscious decisions we make each day – 70 on average – ranging from whether or not to hit the first snooze alarm to determining the punishment for our child for having created a crayon mural on the living room wall. Certainly nothing earth-shattering, but, as we indicated earlier, they do have consequences. The majority of decisions are made in a split second or two, based largely on habit and our perception of how consequential they are. However, many decisions, especially the big ones, can take as long as nine minutes to formulate. That can translate into several mind-numbing hours lost in thought each day. Still, most of us place little weight on these daily decisions in terms of how they might shape our lives. Can you even remember all of the conscious decisions you made today?

Conversely, we are more likely to remember many of the momentous, life-changing decisions we've made – choosing which college to attend, deciding to get married, deciding to have a child, or deciding to buy a house. And, because of their significance, we will most likely be able to look back on them throughout our lives and weigh their consequences. In most cases, these life-event decisions are made when we reach a crossroads that requires a decision and it is often a joint decision involving people who are close to us. Of course, some of these decisions usually take months or even years to formulate following a thorough assessment process.

Somewhere in the middle are those decisions, which by their very nature, can also be life-changing, yet their timing is often dictated by a host of factors including a person's attitude, preferences, knowledge, comfort level, available options, and the perceived level of urgency about the situation. For instance, a birth in the family will trigger a number of immediate, smaller decisions, such as buying furniture for the baby's room and stocking up on diapers. But the more consequential, and potentially life-changing decisions, such as establishing a college savings account or buying additional life insurance, while consciously determined to be of extreme importance, take much longer and are often postponed due to their perceived complexity, at least as compared with deciding which brand of diapers to buy.

But these larger decisions are usually anticipated and made after a period of careful deliberation following the gathering of information and opinions to go along with some soul searching. These decisions can be weighed and measured in ways that enable you to understand the consequences in advance. And, while we can find ourselves regretting a big decision, we can at least see where we went wrong and learn from our mistakes.

That is not so easily done when life gets off track as a consequence of thousands of smaller decisions made over a long period of time. Consider for a moment the great quote from renowned life coach, Wayne Dyer, "Our lives are the sum total of the choices we have made." Think about it. The average adult makes more than 4,000 micro-decisions each day – many unconscious and, perhaps, inconsequential, but in the aggregate, along with all of the bigger decisions we make, they can shape our lives in very profound way.

The average amount of thoughts that a human being has is somewhere around 40,000 to 50,000. This means only 1 in 10 thoughts actually convert to decisions. If we were to increase our conversion ratio, we will be so much more successful. We have often heard that many successful people are very decisive. The reality is that the conversion ratio of their thoughts into decisions is much higher.

The sum total of all of your everyday decisions can be much bigger and much more consequential than any single, monumental decision. So, the question you have to ask is "what kind of life are my daily decisions creating?"

This leads us to the more crucial question of how we actually make the dozens of life-shaping decisions each day. Are they made through deliberation over options and outcomes; or are they made semi-consciously based on the immediate circumstances and emotions of the moment without regard for long-term consequences. Do they contribute to a purpose or vision of how you want to lead your life; or are they reactions spawned from habits which may or may not have been formed by design? Perhaps it's a mixture of both. The question then becomes,

> *"How could my life be different/better/improved if I had more conscious control over my decisions?"*

How Do You Lead Your Life?

For anyone who has any ambition of living a good life based on a clear vision or purpose, this is neither a small nor secret question. The outcomes for people who let their decisions guide them are dramatically different than the outcomes for people who are able to guide their decisions. For the former, their lives are typically engulfed in *Chaos, Confusion, Conflict, Complaints, and Clutter* – also known as the Bad 5 C's of Life; while the latter have a greater capacity to move through life with *Clarity, Confidence, Creativity, Critical Thinking and Conviction* – the Good 5 C's of Life.

At any particular moment in our lives we could be functioning in either world; however, we may or may not immediately recognize on which side we tend to operate; or maybe we bounce between the two. However, not knowing when or how many decisions are made in either mode can be nearly as stifling as the Bad 5 C's of Life itself. Suffice it to say, reasonable and ambitious people would choose to stay on the path of the Good C's if they had the capacity to do so.

How do You Lead Your Life?

The Bad 5 C's of Life	*The Good 5 C's of Life*
Chaos	*Clarity*
Confusion	*Confidence*
Conflict	*Creativity*
Complaining	*Critical Thinking*
Clutter	*Conviction*

By their literal definition, we can see how the Bad C's can manifest themselves as decision killers and killers of Life in General.

Chaos: "a state of complete disorder and confusion."

There's no better way to describe the condition of your mind as it tries to absorb the sheer volume of noise coming at it from 360 degrees, 24/7. Suffice to say, it is not the mind-state from which to make rational, "well-informed" decisions. If your life seems a bit chaotic, it's probably because your mind lacks an effective noise filter – one that is able to distinguish between good and bad information in order to focus on the quality rather than the quantity of information. People who live their lives without a defined purpose tend to lack that essential noise filter.

Confusion: "the state of being confused or perplexed."

Generally, confusion is a by-product of chaos where a choice has to be made between multiple options. Too many choices, and/or information surrounding them, increases the level of uncertainty in any decision, which, in turn, increases the fear of regret, which, in turn, often leads to paralysis or choosing not to choose. When our indecisiveness, over even the smallest decisions, becomes endemic to our behavior, our lives can become even more chaotic.

Conflict: "a psychological state resulting from the often unconscious opposition between simultaneous but incompatible desires, needs, drives, or impulses."

Have you ever decided on a certain course for your life only to find yourself making contrary choices weighed down by ambivalence or even shame? Who hasn't? For me, it came when I decided to change my diet and cut out sugary and fatty foods. I felt my willpower was strong, but there were so many instances when friends and family insisted I make an exception "just this once." Each exception, and, thankfully, there weren't that many, only worsen the "love-hate" relationship I had with food, increasing the likelihood that I might veer off course. Decisions not weighed by values, beliefs, and clearly defined goals can lead to a conflicted state of mind which is unpleasant at best, and potentially emotionally crippling at worst.

Complaining: "expressing discontent or unhappiness about a situation."

Why do we complain? On a trivial level we complain everyday – it's too hot or too cold, the line's too long or too slow, the service here is horrible, he's not doing it right, etc. These are often reflexive, mostly unconscious reactions triggered by short fuses and frustration, and, for the most part, they are perfectly normal human expressions; except, perhaps, if it's a chronic condition. Chronic complainers or, people who complain about a lot in life tend to form their decisions while looking through a prism of discontent, focused on what's lacking in their lives versus a positive outlook.

Clutter: "a condition of disorderliness or overcrowding."

Typically, when we think of *clutter*, we tend to imagine papers, books and stuff piled like an archeological dig on our workspace. Some would argue that such disarray makes it very difficult to work productively. Now imagine such disarray occurring in your mind. Physical clutter tends to fill the void left by the absence of discipline, priorities and a plan, and mental clutter is no different.

For those faced with clutter might counter that it was none other than Albert Einstein who said, "If a cluttered desk signs a cluttered mind, of what, and then is an empty desk a sign?" However, the clutter of chaos, confusion, conflict and discontent may not be what he had in mind.

Clearly, when we spend any amount of time wallowing in the Bad C's of life, our decision-making is hampered; and, at its bad, we postpone or decide not to decide which is far worse in many respects than having made a bad decision at all. Indecision can only compound the magnitude of unrealized, smaller decisions. Left to intense, small issues accumulate and become bigger issues to the point when a decision is made for you either by someone who has undesired control of the issue (a boss, a creditor, a family member, etc.), or after you have backed yourself into a corner with no other option but to decide. In either case, the outcome is likely to be far unfavorable than just about any small decision you could have made along the way.

Bad decisions, made when they are still small, are often correctable, sometimes even retractable leaving a minimal residue of harm; and there is usually an opportunity to learn, adjust and recover with a better decision. However, once they combine into big, consequential decisions, the outcomes can be more far-reaching than you could have possibly anticipated and it is far more difficult to minimize their impact. And, the only thing you can learn from forcing a bad, big decision is that you probably could have avoided it by making the tough, smaller decisions when they first presented themselves.

In Pursuit of Clarity, Confidence and Conviction

Decision-making is difficult enough without the encumbrance of chaos, confusion and conflict, so why do we allow these conditions to infiltrate our lives when it is far easier and more constructive when we operate with clarity, confidence, and conviction using creativity and critical thinking? Because we are human! Let's go with that – mainly because it's true. While it is true that humans are capable of rational thought at the highest level of consciousness, we are also naturally bound to our instinctive behavior, which is constantly reinforced by our emotions.

Fear, hope, love, hate, envy, empathy, pride, shame – all powerful emotions, operate freely within our psyche to influence our behavior allowing us to suspend for a moment, or, in some cases, for a lifetime, any rational thought. When our minds are powered by emotions, they become more penetrable by the chaos, confusion and conflict that can then dominate our lives – for a moment, or for a lifetime.

To have clarity, confidence and conviction in our decision-making requires us to be able to overpower our emotions with rational thought, and that requires an abundance of discipline. The ability to exercise self-discipline in the face of challenging circumstances doesn't come naturally for most people. But those who are able to do so are better able to inoculate themselves from all of the noise and cut through the chaos that often clouds their judgment.

Because the exercise of discipline is a conscious action, it needs to be reinforced by certain beliefs that the action will lead to the best possible outcome. Disciplined people accept the fact that there is risk in any decision, and the chance of experiencing negative outcome is a very real likelihood. But, by weighing the options against all possible outcomes, they also know that to do nothing at all can produce the worst possible outcome.

Disciplined decision makers are generally confident that when they do decide, it means it was the right decision at the time with the information they had available. So, for them, it only becomes a wrong decision when unknowns surface and the worst case is they simply make another decision. Regardless, by making a decision, they force an outcome, which reveals any unknowns that can be incorporated into future decisions.

Of course, exercising disciplined decision-making while eliminating the demons of chaos and confusion is not easy for most people, which is why I have introduced the *Decision Simplifier*™, a reliable and easy to use tool that can not only simplify your life, it can also be a source of daily empowerment. Discipline, which is elusive to many people, is the adherence to those things that have most reliably worked, and the *Decision Simplifier*™ is a proven process for taking control of the everyday decisions that can shape your life.

Systems to implement as a habit
when applicable to your situation:

I. Dealing with Chaos:
    1. Discover from the workshop how chaos is created.
    2. Learn the secrets of dissecting the chaos from the workshop and connecting to solutions that will help you eliminate the chaos.
    3. With help from the workshop, learn the three hidden secrets to help you eliminate chaos and build strategies and activities that will help you deal with chaos on an ongoing basis.

Eliminate Chaos in life with The Chaos Eliminator™ workshop at http://www.BizActionCoach.com/product/the-chaos-eliminator/

II. Removing Confusion:
    1. Narrow down your most viable choices.

2. From the workshop, discover the secret of dissecting the options.
3. With help from the workshop, learn the hidden ways to build on one choice and implement it.

Eradicate confusion with The Confusion Destroyer™ workshop at http://www.BizActionCoach.com/product/the-confusion-destroyer/

III. Removing Clutter:
1. Identify all the areas in your life where you see clutter.
2. Through the workshop, discover the hidden truths on how to eliminate majority of the clutter in all those areas.
3. Build a list of activities and habits you need to develop to start eliminating clutter from your life.

Bring cleanliness and structure The Clutter Remover™ workshop at http://www.BizActionCoach.com/product/the-clutter-remover/

IV. Stop Complaining:
1. Make a list of top 5 complaints you normally make.
2. Through the workshop, discover how to resolve the complaints you are making or eliminating the need to complain.
3. With help from workshop, learn the secret of communication techniques that will make you a complaint-free individual.

Resolve complaints with The Complaint Resolver™ System workshop at http://www.BizActionCoach.com/product/the-complaint-resolver-2/

V. System to destroy conflict:
   1. Ask yourself who are you trying to resolve conflict with – is it with yourself or someone else?
   2. If it is someone else, try getting The Friction Destroyer™ DVD to help you resolve the conflict in an amicable way. If it is your own self, let the workshop help you discover the hidden ways to resolve frictions with your own self.
   3. Develop and implement at least one to three activities derived from the workshop.

Reduce day-to-day conflict with The Friction Destroyer™ DVD at http://www.BizActionCoach.com/product/friction-destroyer/

Get the entire deck of cards (52 Cards-52 Systems) at http://www.BizActionCoach.com/product/the-deck-of-cards-workshop-system/

Please complete the exercise on the next page before proceeding to read the next chapter.

What thought or thoughts come to your mind after reading this chapter?

_____

_____

_____

_____

_____

_____

_____

What Decision or Decisions have you made about the thought or thoughts you had?

_____

_____

_____

_____

_____

_____

_____

What Growth Actions would you take today or by a specific date to implement your thoughts?

_____

_____

_____

_____

_____

_____

_____

A True Story

I have always made the decision to make the hardest choices as they tend to deliver the highest rewards in the long run. When I graduated from college I had more than a dozen job offers and majority of them were with a good starting fixed salary for a college graduate. I rejected all of them and went with starting my own business. Ever since, I have never worked for anyone else besides myself and the rewards have been far better. Since then, every time, I have opted for the harder choices that push me to another level in my personal and professional life. I learned early on in college that Successful people do the things others don't like to do. This has kept me out of my comfort zone.

Chapter 4

how to simplify
your daily decisions

r ecently, psychologists have begun to study how people's
attitudes affect their decision-making. They have found
that some people tend to view the world in more black
and white terms, and, for them, their choices are clearer. Black-
and-white thinkers tend to be driven by a clearly defined sense
of purpose that guides their decision making. Their choices are
starker; often portrayed in "right" and "wrong" terms in which
the alternatives can be quickly narrowed to the one or two that
are aligned with their purpose and that will produce the greatest
good for themselves as well as the world around them.

Black-and white thinkers are characterized by quick
decision-making, higher productivity and, generally, a more

positive outlook on life. This is not to say they don't make mistakes; they do. However, their sense of purpose, positive outlook and faith in the future allows them to quickly learn from their mistakes and convert them into decisions that lead to a better outcome.

The research has found, however, that most people tend to see the world in shades of gray, and, for them the choices are never as clear. Shades-of-gray thinkers are more inclined to have conflicting feelings about situations which traps them in a constant state of ambivalence. Certainly, ambivalence can be a positive trait in some of its forms. Introspection, prudence, and seeking counsel are attributes common to most successful people. However, it can also be the biggest obstacle to resolving a problem or achieving success in any circumstance. While it may be OK to be a shades-of-gray thinker in terms of world views, it can have the effect of restricting progress or worsening problems on a personal or business level.

In an increasingly complex world where important issues can become muddled with politics and contradictions, many people like the fact that they're a shades-of-gray thinker. Some would say this has given rise to the powerful "independent" voter block which doesn't seem to view the issues of the day as simply black and white. They're more apt to waver on supporting any side of an argument until they've completely exhausted their study of the issue. However, when it comes to making personal or business decisions, such ambivalence may do more harm than good.

The good news is that shades-of-gray thinkers rarely make hasty decisions because they tend to over-think rather than under-think. The bad news is they also tend to procrastinate or avoid decisions to the point where the consequences of a non-decision can be as detrimental.

Often times, they prolong their decision-making in a quest for the "perfect" decision – one that can only result in the perfect outcome; but, perfectionism in decision-making is not really possible. People who prolong their decision-making for fear of making a mistake are less likely to achieve success.

How to Become a Black and White Decision-Maker

If it is true that thinking in black-and-white can produce better personal and business decisions more easily, is it possible for people whose default thought process is set on gray to simply flip the switch to black-and-white? The answer lies, in part, with the Habits to Happiness mapped out in Chapter 3 in which we discussed, in depth, how the traits and attributes of happy people enable them to more easily make decisions with clarity and confidence.

Central to this enhanced ability to make decisions is that people who enjoy contentment in their lives tend to have a clear definition of their ambition for a good life – defined by a greater sense of purpose and supporting priorities. Their vision and their goals are based on deeply felt values and beliefs which they use as a compass in determining their direction. They know what they need and want that will feed their happiness, and they know what will detract from it. To a great extent, happy people are more likely to think in black and white terms when it comes to making decisions of any consequence.

Conversely, if you view your life in shades of gray and don't know where you're going, or why, then risks may not be worth taking, challenges become barriers and indecision and doubt will cloud your future. Without a clear vision and goals, you are more likely to conflate the pursuit of happiness with the pursuit of more which can never bring true fulfillment.

Making the transformation to a life of happiness requires taking action, the type that leads to positive results and gets you closer to your vision of a good life. In order to take action, you need to be able to make clear and deliberate decisions. Indecisiveness is the enemy of change and the supporter of fear and doubt.

The power of decisiveness gives you the ability to move beyond the excuses that prevent you from changing any aspect of your life at the most critical time, which is the present. With experience, you learn very quickly that the risk of a bad decision is much more preferable than the enduring dread of indecision.

Building the Habit of Black and White Thinking

For the majority of people who are shades-of-gray thinkers, it may be possible to, every now and then, simply flip the switch and become a black-and-white thinker; especially if a decision has to be made concerning an issue that is near and dear to their hearts – an issue for which they have a high level of clarity and conviction. As we've discussed in previous chapters, developing desired habits comes easier when you can identify the traits you are trying to develop or change.

In this case, becoming more decisive, with confidence and conviction in your decisions, is a trait black-and-white thinkers share. Whether it's instinctive or a trait developed over time, there are certain key habits performed by black-and-white thinkers that can be learned and mastered by anyone looking to permanently flip the switch. I've distilled these habits into a simple technique to be employed as you approach any significant decision.

It's called the P-A-E-D method:

P – Purpose: Have a clear purpose in life – a vision for what you want to accomplish; a conviction in your beliefs; values that guide you. Write it all down and turn it into a daily mantra. The more clearly defined your purpose, the more quickly you can narrow down your choices.

A – Alternative: The more quickly you can narrow down your choices, the more quickly you will identify the alternative that will serve your purpose.

E – Emotional State-of-Mind: Is the decision being forced on you by stress or any emotional turbulence? If so, pause, take a step back, focus on your purpose, and evaluate the alternatives with calm and confidence.

D – Doing the Most Good: Will your decision result in an outcome that brings the greatest good to the greatest number of people, including yourself; or will it simply result in doing the least amount of harm. Which better serves your purpose – doing the most good possible or doing the least amount of harm?

While it may not be possible, or even appropriate, to apply the PAED method to all of your decisions, by consciously framing important decisions around it, you have a greater likelihood of forming your decision more quickly with confidence and conviction. Copy it down and try it on your next big decision.

Choose Happiness with the Decision Simplifier™ Mobile Application

The key is to systematize your decision-making in a way that emphasizes your objectivity and compartmentalizes your emotions. Anything that prompts a thoughtful decision-making process is always better than letting decisions languish in the brain. However, what I found is that, while these tools appropriately call for listing pros and cons or tradeoffs, they tend to allow our biases to enter the process. The end result is an outcome that is likely to be slanted toward our preconceived notions or feelings.

That's why I created the **Decision Simplifier™ Mobile Application**— a simple 30 second productivity tool for bringing clarity to your decisions with minimal influence from your biases or the range of emotions that typically accompany a decision. Essentially, the Decision Simplifier™ Mobile Application enables you to compartmentalize your objectivity and filter out any biases. Its sole purpose is to keep you focused on what will increase your happiness or detract from it.

While the Decision Simplifier™ can't prevent you from making wrong decisions, the process will bring a level of clarity that will enable you to more quickly learn from your mistakes and make appropriate adjustments with greater confidence.

Of course, the key to making the Decision Simplifier an effective solution is to follow through on the result even if your instinct tells you it may be wrong. Remember, your "instinct" is often shaped by your emotions, biases, and the character traits you may be trying to change.

The Decision Simplifier™ Mobile Application provides the thorough thought process you think is needed; but it does what is important, which is to help you filter all of the influences out of the process and bring clarity, confidence and conviction to your decision. And, in that you can trust.

Systems to implement as a habit when applicable to your situation:

I. Developing Black and White Decision Making:
    1. Write down one to five decisions that you had postponed in the last week.
    2. With the help of the workshop, discover the secret of how to eliminate procrastination on decision making.
    3. From the workshop, Build a customized list of activities, habits or discipline you will implement to be a black and white decision maker.

Bring Clarity in your decision making with The Black and White Decision Maker™ workshop at http://www.BizActionCoach.com/product/the-black-and-white-decision-maker/

II. Aiming for Success rather than perfectionism:
    1. Write down one to three tasks that you have been aiming for perfectionism and right next to that task

write down what tasks or projects have you postponed as a result of aiming for perfection.

2. From the workshop, discover the hidden ways on putting major projects in motion and achieving progress along the way.

3. Build a system of achieving projects and use that for every project that you will work on.

Achieve your projects in record time with The Strategic Project Achiever™ workshop at http://www.BizActionCoach.com/product/the-strategic-project-achiever/

III. Narrowing down your alternates in decisions you have to make:

1. Write down the decision that you feel has a lot of options that you need to narrow down.

2. From the workshop, discover ways to narrow down your choices and connecting to your purpose.

3. Use the worksheet in the workshop until you have arrived at the One Alternate.

Please check out The One Alternate Developer™ workshop at http://www.BizActionCoach.com/product/the-one-alternate-developer/

IV. Developing Calmness:

1. Write down one to three situations in the last 7 days where you completely lost calmness.

2. What was the end result of your losing calmness and control and were you happy with it?

3. With help from the workshop discover the simple hidden ways to build calmness as a habit and build a list of activities that you discipline yourself to do it to build calmness.

Powerfully resolve situations with The Calmness Habit™ workshop at http://www.BizActionCoach.com/product/the-calmness-habit/

V. Doing the most good in any situation:

1. Write down the one decision you feel is the hardest to make.

2. With the steps and process identified in the workshop, discover the secret to do the most good in the situation to all those involved.

3. Make that decision.

Discover the most good for all with The "Most Good" Decision Making System™ workshop at http://www.BizActionCoach.com/product/the-most-good-decision-making/

Get the entire deck of cards (52 Cards-52 Systems) at http://www.BizActionCoach.com/product/the-deck-of-cards-workshop-system/

Chapter Workbook Assignment

- Download the Rajparth Mobile App to your Smart Phone – it's available for both Android and iPhone devices.
- Think of a big decision you made in the last couple of days and apply the Decision Simplifier™ Mobile **Application** to see how the decision pans out. Did it validate your decision? If not, consider whether you would have made a different decision had you used the Decision Simplifier™
- Think of decision you have to make and use the Decision Simplifier **App**. Consider how the result makes you feel? Confident? Clear in your conviction? If not, explore the emotion you are feeling about the result and why you feel uncomfortable.
- Make a habit of using the Decision Simplifier use it at least three times during the course of the day – for your decisions.
- Share the Decision Simplifier with your spouse, your children, your staff or team at work. Conduct a brief workshop and encourage its use.

Please complete the exercise on the next page before proceeding to read the next chapter.

What thought or thoughts come to your mind after reading this chapter?

_____

_____

_____

_____

_____

_____

_____

What Decision or Decisions have you made about the thought or thoughts you had?

_____

_____

_____

_____

_____

_____

_____

What Growth Actions would you take today or by a specific date to implement your thoughts?

_____

_____

_____

_____

_____

_____

_____

A True Story

In the first year on the business, right out of college, I had a goal to make six figure income or quit forever. I had a commitment to myself that if I make that goal, I would shave off my moustache and continue to be self-employed. I surpassed my goal, shaved off my moustache, and was honored in Time Magazine and Sports Illustrated by the companies I did business with.

This was a result of clear black and white thinking with a die-hard commitment. I now have that die-hard commitment to the world to provide Security from Enemies of Prosperity™ and build a high achiever in you.

Chapter 5

simplifying your most important financial decisions

inancial decisions of any type can be overwhelming and confusing. Faced with seemingly unlimited choices, people can become paralyzed from fear of making the wrong choice leading to procrastination or complete inaction. Resistance to change is another emotion – a subset of fear or self-doubt – that can lead to financial apathy. Our comfort zones may seem like a safe place to be, but we can't hide from all of the elements around us that can turn us into sitting ducks. In fact, in our individual pursuits of wealth, each of us is waging a battle against powerful elements that have the potential to take away that which we've worked hard to attain. And, any indecision or inaction will virtually ensure our defeat.

> *"It is said that if you know your enemies and know yourself, you will not be endangered in a hundred battles; if you do not know your enemies but do know yourself, you will win one and lose one; if you do not know your enemies nor yourself, you will be defeated in every single battle."*
> —**Sun Tzu**, *the Art of War*

Confronting the Enemies of Wealth

Unbeknownst to most people, the pursuit of financial success takes place on a timeless battlefield upon which largely unseen enemies engage us every day in a perpetual assault on our wealth. These enemies of wealth, which exist both externally and internally, are omnipotent, omnipresent, and unrelenting, yet many people are oblivious to their existence. They thrive on the financial vacuum created by indecision and inaction; and they see procrastination as an opportunity to pounce on our assets. The damage they inflict is gradual and subtle, so it's not easily detectable while it's occurring, but it can have a devastating affect over the long term. These enemies of wealth will never go away; they will always be engaging you in battle; however, with the right counter-offensive, you can mitigate their impact, and, in the long-term, emerge victorious.

What are these enemies of wealth?

Lack of Discipline – It's impossible to accumulate wealth if you spend more money than you earn. Even if you don't, you really can't know if you will be financially successful if you don't track where your money is going. Discipline is not an inherent human trait; however, without it, we are destined to fail financially.

Debt – Some financial planners would argue that debt has no peer as an enemy of wealth. Unquestionably, carrying costly debt is the biggest obstacle to achieving financial independence.

Taxes – While it is our responsibility to pay taxes, we are under no obligation to pay more than is absolutely necessary. Yet, most people are unaware of how much in taxes they pay or the impact of unnecessary taxes on their ability to accumulate wealth.

Inflation – Inflation is the stealthiest enemy of all; and, while you may not notice its effect today or tomorrow, it has the potential to take away a significant portion of your purchasing power over time. Even at the low inflation rates of today (around 3 percent) your assets will lose half their value in 24 years.

Behavioral Mistakes – When it comes to investing, most people are their own enemy. More specifically, it's allowing our emotions to guide investment decisions, which, more often than not, leads to behavioral mistakes, such as trying to time the markets, trying to pick the winners, chasing returns, or following the herd – all of which can be extremely costly.

Life Unexpected – Life happens, and it's full of the unexpected which can be very costly. A job loss, an illness, accidents, a death in the family, legal complications can happen at any time. Most people are not fully prepared for the unexpected and the financial consequences can be devastating.

Unintended Heirs – Most people want their children and future generations to benefit from their life's work; however, without a properly planned estate, the state could decide who gets your assets, and the federal government could become your biggest heir.

On their own, each of these enemies of wealth, left unchecked, could become impairment to building wealth. But, collectively, without the proper strategy to engage them, they will not only prevent you from accumulating wealth, they can potentially devastate you financially. Fortunately, ammunition and fortification are available; however, you need a battle plan with strategies targeting each of these enemies.

You Need a Financial Plan to Battle the "Enemies of Wealth"

In facing down our financial adversaries, the only fortification that can ensure success is a well-conceived, comprehensive financial plan. In fact, when we have clearly defined goals and priorities backed by thoughtful strategies with specific action plans, we have the only weaponry needed to effectively turn back their unceasing assault on our ability to build wealth. Of course, that also assumes that we have the discipline and strength to stick with the plan.

Set Clearly Defined Goals

One of the best illustrated instances of indecision occurs in the story of Alice in Wonderland in which Alice comes to a fork in the road and must choose a path to continue her journey. She seeks the advice of grinning Cheshire cat which appears out of nowhere. "Where are you headed?" The cat asks Alice where she was headed, to which she replied, "I don't know." "Well," the cat responds, "then it really doesn't matter." With no clear destination or goals, it's impossible to make decisions with any degree of clarity and any path we choose will be paved with uncertainty. Setting well-defined financial goals that include a clear vision of what you want to achieve and a time horizon for achieving it, is essential if you ever expect to achieve it.

Equally important, goals tell you where you are. One of the reasons people stumble in their financial pursuits is they can't see their progress and they quit in discouragement or out of fear of failure. Goals can be broken down into checkpoints or benchmarks that enable you to see if you are on track.

Most importantly, clearly defined goals will help you clarify your choices. If a road won't take you to your destination, you don't take it. Your choices become clear, your decisions and actions have purpose, and your results bring more satisfaction. Goals are the pathway to your financial success, and goal setting is the crucial first step:

1. Inventory your needs and wants. So much to do, so little time. Do a brain dump in a sheet of paper of everything you need and want to do financially. Make a separate list for needs and wants.

2. Determine time horizon. Separate your priorities into short-term and long-term goals. Assign a specific time frame to each.

> Short-term = 1 to 5 years
> Intermediate-term = 5 to 10 years
> Long-term = 10+ years

3. Prioritize. Go through your list and assign a numerical rating with "1" being most important. On a separate sheet, write down your top three needs, followed by your top three wants. Needs should always take precedence over wants.

4. Determine its cost. Estimate how much it will cost if you had to pay for the goal today. You will need to calculate the monthly savings requirement for each goal.

5. Visualize the outcome. Beginning with your top priority, take moment to visualize the goal as if you have already achieved it. Note how it makes you feel. The stronger the emotion you have about a goal, the more likely it is you will achieve it. This exercise often leads to a reprioritization of your goals.

6. Establish milestones. Each goal should be broken down into smaller goals with milestone dates. You will find that a goal is easier to pursue when you have smaller, more frequent targets to shoot for. Achieving short-term milestones produces more motivation.

7. Develop action plans. Create a separate action plan for each goal including specific steps, timing, milestones, and a tracking log. Include any steps you will need to take to educate yourself on a type of savings or investment program.

8. Hold Yourself Accountable. Share your goals and action plans with your spouse, your family, a trusted friend. Ask them to check in with you periodically about your progress.

With clearly defined goals, you will not only have greater clarity in your financial decision-making; you will be able to develop targeted strategies and action plans for fending off the enemies of wealth.

The Best Defense is a Good Offense

Next, you'll need to develop some detailed strategies and action plans for achieving your goals; however, in doing so, it is vitally important to take the measure of each of your enemies and how they can act to thwart your plan. The only option to successfully defend against the enemies of wealth is to go on the offense. Your financial strategies should be designed with the understanding that the threat of an attack by any one of these enemies, while maybe not imminent, is inevitable, and that to ignore them would increase your risk exposure dramatically. Your strategies, therefore, become premeditated acts that aim to eliminate the threat.

Enemy #1 – A Lack of Discipline

Discipline or the lack thereof, is the enemy that resides within; specifically, the lack of discipline over our finances. In this digital age, we have become creatures of instant gratification where information and commerce now travel at digital speed, and many people have lost their ability to control their impulses.

Discipline is the exercise of the mind to do the right thing by staying the course. If you have a budget plan and it calls for spending $100 less on leisure activities so you can save $100 more each month, the exercise of discipline becomes the conscious action to follow through with the plan. Without discipline, we are more likely to spend the money, forego savings for the month, and, if we overspend, dip into our savings to cover the shortfall. It's one of the biggest reasons why people fail to get ahead. In the long run, it becomes the enemy of your financial success.

Human nature being the way it is we often need reinforcement to maintain and exercise discipline. An effective system is easy to set up, easy to manage, and it provides you with easy mechanisms for tracking, measuring and accountability.

When done right, the most effective system for reinforcing financial discipline is a budget, also referred to as "a spending plan". Budgets that are unrealistic or too difficult to manage are quickly swapped out for good intentions. However, budgets or spending plans that reflect your reality while providing a realistic path to improving your cash flow, can not only be motivating, they can be liberating, freeing you from having to make difficult choices.

Budgeting is not very complicated. In fact, with four easy steps, you can structure a budget that is easy to follow:

1. Establish spending priorities around your most important financial goals (i.e., pay off debt, build an emergency fund; save for retirement).

2. Establish a clear spending goal for your priorities. If your cash flow is limited, target your top priority first. (i.e., to save $500 a month towards a $6,000 emergency fund). This will be your first expenditure each month.

3. With the remaining cash flow, itemize all expenditures in two main categories – Essential and Non-essential.

Begin with essentials such as mortgage/rent, taxes, food, transportation, personal need, debt. Then allocate the balance of your cash flow among non-essential items, such as dining out, leisure activities, household items, clothing, etc.

4. You can create your budget on a paper spread sheet, and Excel spreadsheet, or you can use one of many free personal finance websites, such as Mint.com. The latter is strongly recommended because it's simple and tracking can be automated by linking it to your bank account for real time tracking and easy management.

After structuring your budget, success comes down to how well you manage it. Certainly, the more you can automate it (via online tools), the less hands-on you need to be. But, for even more effective cash flow management, we can learn some lessons from successful businesses which must manage their cash flow effectively or die.

Managing Your Cash Flow like a Business

What we know about successful companies is that they manage their cash flow based on allocation – they allocate their cash to various accounts so it can be managed according to different objectives. Generally, a company will have a cash-on-hand account to cover immediate cash needs; a working capital account to cover ongoing operating expenses; and a long-term account to save for future capital investments. Each account is managed separately according to specific guidelines established through a budget, so financial decisions are almost all automatic. The only way anything changes, is by restructuring the budget which might be done as part of the company's annual planning.

Now imagine yourself as a company. What would be the benefit of structuring your budget around three different accounts, each with specific guidelines for their use? Too complicated? If you think about it, you're already doing it, except you're trying to manage all three in your head, which is why most people suffer from muddled brains when trying to make basic financial decisions.

The goal is to simplify; and the best way to do that is by breaking your budget down into smaller, more manageable pieces. And, if you think about these pieces as "compartments" or "buckets," it becomes easier to manage them according to their objective or purpose. Your spending objectives will be more clearly defined, and, by having separate guidelines for each account, your financial decisions are practically made for you.

Here's how I advise my clients to structure their budgets:

Lifestyle Account™

Your Lifestyle Account is a bank checking account used to pay everyone besides yourself.

<u>What goes in?</u>

The amount you have determined in your budget for covering your lifestyle expenses. Remember, effective cash flow management requires that you first establish a savings goal (for businesses, it's a profit goal), then budget everything else around that.

<u>What goes out</u>?

All essential and non-essential expenditure. If you budget effectively, this account should be empty by the end of the month. If you have managed to live below your means, any surplus cash should be moved to your Planning Account or Wage Account.

<u>Planning Account</u>™

Your Planning Account is a bank checking or savings account that houses the funds you have earmarked for savings and investment towards your financial goals.

<u>What goes in</u>?

The amount you have established as a savings goal over and above the funds you contribute automatically to an employer-sponsored retirement plan. Any excess funds available from under-spending in your Life Style Account should also go into this account

<u>What goes out</u>?

Money needed to secure your family's future. Retirement goal, family protection needs, such as life insurance, disability insurance, long-term care, and other important financial goals.

<u>Wage Account (Emergency Fund)</u>

This is called a Wage Account because your wages, up to six months' worth, is protected from creditors (with some exceptions). Also, should your income ever be interrupted, this account will be the source of your wages to cover living expenses until your income resumes.

<u>What goes in</u>?

The amount you have established as a savings goal each month until you have built your cash reserve. It's recommended you have a minimum of six month's worth of living expenses saved in your emergency fund.

<u>What goes out</u>?

Funds needed to cover necessary expenses not covered by your Lifestyle Account, such as major car repairs or living expenses in the event of an interruption in your income.

Enemy #2 – Debt

It's virtually impossible to go through life without incurring any debt. The issue becomes whether we are in control of our debt. For people who lack discipline and spend impulsively, chances are their debt will control them at some point. If we are in control of our debt, it's because we can afford to carry it, it doesn't interfere with our ability to meet our lifestyle needs or our ability to achieve our financial goals; and we have a plan to pay it off. There are two fundamental rules of thumb to determine whether you are in control of your debt, or you are on the verge of losing control:

Rule # 1: Debt to Liquidity Ratio:

At a minimum, you should maintain at least 10 percent liquidity to debt. If you can, 25 percent is preferable. For example, if you own four properties and the debt on all properties totals one million, you should at a minimum have at least $100,000 between all the liquidity sources. Liquidity can come in many forms, such as your checking accounts, savings accounts, business checking and savings accounts, investment accounts, loan available through 401K accounts, and cash value life insurance.

Rule # 2: Good Debt versus Bad Debt:

As a general rule debt such as a home loan, student loan or business loan with low to moderate (less than 8 percent) interest rates can be considered good debt as long as you apply Rule #1 (Liquidity Ratio). Consumer debt, typically in the form of credit card debt or installment loans, is considered bad debt and should never exist. Credit cards can play an important role in personal finances – building good credit, paying for unexpected expenses, controlling expenses – if they are used wisely and balances are paid in full each month. But, credit card debt, when incurred from impulse purchases or a lack of discipline can easily spiral out of control.

If your debt is beginning to interfere with your lifestyle needs or financial goals, you should immediately make debt payoff your priority, shifting your cash flow allocation from other objectives.

Enemy # 3 – Taxes

Contrary to what some politicians want you to believe, it is not your patriotic duty to pay more in taxes than is absolutely necessary. Even in a famous case before the U.S. Court of Appeals (ultimately decided against a taxpayer), we are instructed by the Judge (Learned Hand) that, "Anyone may so arrange his affairs that his taxes shall be as low as possible; he is not bound to choose that pattern which will best pay the Treasury; there is not even a patriotic duty to increase one's taxes."

With over 74,000 pages, the U.S. Tax Code is beyond the capacity of most human beings to understand. The Tax Code challenges all taxpayers to avail themselves of whatever tax break they might find. The problem is that, most people have neither the time, nor the inclination to become tax experts which is why Americans leave billions of dollars in tax breaks on the table each year.

In order to ensure you are paying the least necessary tax, you should be working, at a minimum, with a tax professional. However, as you climb the income or wealth ladder, your tax planning may need to involve a team of professionals, headed by a Certified Public Accountant. Your particular plan may involve tax reduction strategies that require the assistance of an attorney, an independent financial advisor and an independent insurance professional. Forming a team of professionals such as this can be a daunting task, which is why you should consider working with an independent financial advisor who employs a team approach in working with professional advisors from all of the planning disciplines.

While, on the surface, the collective advice of a team of professional may seem like a costly way to go, if your situation is one that requires it, you are very likely to save a multiple of the cost in taxes; and, more importantly, stay out of the crosshairs of the IRS while do so.

Three-Bucket Tax Diversification Strategy

Most people can benefit from diversifying the tax treatment of their long-term investments. By employing the "three-bucket" tax strategy, you can create better tax treatment of your income while increasing your flexibility in the use of your assets.

A tax-diversified investment strategy includes a mix three buckets – and here's why:

With tax-free vehicles, *what you receive as income is what you get. You don't pay any taxes when it is received. However, you also didn't benefit from any tax deductions when you contribute to the investment.*

For instance, with a Roth IRA, your investments grow tax deferred, and, after age 59 ½, they can be withdrawn tax-free; however, your contributions are made with after-tax dollars.

With the tax-deferred vehicles, *such as a 401k or a Traditional IRA, you were able to deduct your contributions from your income, saving you money at the time, but, upon withdrawal, your funds will be taxed at your ordinary tax rate.*

With taxable vehicles, *you receive no tax deduction and, depending on the type of investment, you pay taxes on interest or on capital gains as they were earned. Interest income is taxed at ordinary tax rates, while long-term capital gains are taxed at 25 percent. Of course, you don't pay any taxes on unrealized capital gains, so, in essence, your investment portfolio can also be a tax-deferred vehicle if you never sell your stocks. But even when you do, you can use losses in your portfolio to offset the gain and reduce your tax.*

As you can see, with some vehicles you can generate significant tax savings currently which can be invested. With some vehicles you forgo current tax savings in order to reap tax savings later. And with some, you may have to pay taxes as you go or when you draw from them in retirement, but it's at a more favorable tax rate.

Enemy #4 – Inflation

Inflation has always been the unbeatable opponent of retirees because of its effect on their standard of living, though its impact on people who retired in the 1950s, 60's and 70's was less significant for a few reasons. First, life expectancies were shorter, generally lasting 10 to 15 years in retirement, which didn't allow for extended inflation creep. Second, the majority of workers who retired in those decades received an income from employer pensions, many of which were indexed for inflation.

Third, interest rates on savings more closely correlated with inflation which lessened the erosion of future purchasing power.

Today's retirees face a new set of problems with regards to inflation. Because guaranteed pension plans are generally a thing of the past, retirees must rely on their own capital to generate sufficient income for their extended lifetimes. Not only must they be able to accumulate capital at a rate that exceeds inflation, they must be able to sustain a rate of growth on their capital throughout their lifetime that exceeds inflation.

Moreover, in the current economic environment, interest rates on savings vehicles are not correlating with the true rate of inflation. Today, savers are actually earning negative rates of return when the actual rate of inflation is factored in.

Finally, because we are living much longer than previous generations, inflation has a much more significant impact on purchasing power when assets and earnings are exposed to it for 20 or 30 years. Even a modest rate of inflation of 3% will cut purchasing power nearly in half over a 20 year period.

Enemy #5 – Behavioral Mistakes

When it comes to investing, people can be their own enemy. Nearly all of the mistakes made by investors can be attributed to their behavior which is typically dictated by their emotions. Fear and greed have a way of driving even the most rational people to making investing decision which is why most investors typically underperform the markets. According to a study by DALBAR, the returns most investors experience lag the actual returns of the mutual funds they buy. For example, over the 20 year period ending in 2013, the S&P 500 index returned 9.22%, but the average equity fund investor only earned 5.02%.

Another DALBAR study found that, over a ten-year period ending in 2010, the average investor has missed out on 60 percent of the stock market's gains. Why? DALBAR concludes that investors are at their worst when the market does poorly, selling once they have a big paper loss and then sitting on the sidelines until the markets have recovered their value. Therefore, they tend to participate in the market primarily when it is in retreat and miss the market when it is on the rise.

Among the many behavioral mistakes investors make are:

Trying to time the market:
While it's not impossible, few investors have been able to move in and out of the market at the right time consistently enough that they gain any significant advantage over the buy-and-hold crowd. Morningstar estimates that the returns on portfolios that tried to time the market over the last decade underperformed the average return on equity funds by 1.5 percent during that period, and that includes several years of negative returns. To do better, investors would need to have called the market shift seven out of ten times, a feat that true timing pros have a hard time matching.

Trying to pick the winners:
Over a five-year period, from 2006 to 2010, only 48 percent of managers of large-cap funds were able to beat the S&P 500. The vast majority of them barely edged out the index. It gets worse for portfolio managers who focus on the international markets – only 18 percent managed to outperform the international index. What this means, is that in that period of time, if you had simply invested in an S&P 500 index fund, which required no active portfolio management (so, you wouldn't have paid the 2 percent investment management fee), you would have earned a better return than more than half of the portfolio managers.

Reacting to short-term events:
The behavioral instinct of humans to "do something" in reaction to extreme events, or the constant barrage of the

media is a survival mechanism that tends to work against us in the investment sphere. Studies have shown that the more often one changes one's portfolio, or, for that matter, even looks at it, the lower will be the return. When investors shift their focus away from their long-term objectives to short-term performance, the results are almost always negative. Leading Warren Buffet to quip, "The stock market is a highly efficient mechanism for the transfer of wealth from the impatient to the patient."

Market crashes, financial meltdowns, Middle East wars, and tsunamis are all consequential to our lives in the moment; however, their impact on the markets over a 20- or 30-year period is so minimal as to cause nothing more than a tiny blip on your long-term investment performance.

Whether investing for retirement or any other objective, the biggest mistake many people make is not having a sound investment strategy in place to guide their decisions. The challenge in investing is not that it takes special skills or knowledge; it's that it is often driven by emotions which can be devastating for investors who lack a clear investment strategy along with the patience and discipline to follow it.

It must start with a goal, a targeted objective with a specific time horizon so you can determine how much you need to invest, what rate of return is needed on your investment and how much risk you will need to take in order to achieve that rate of return. Then, with the help of a trusted, independent investment advisor, you need to construct a properly diversified investment portfolio allocated across several asset classes that reflects your specific objective for growth for the next 15 to 20 years. The only time you should buy or sell any securities after that is when your investment objective changes (which should be rare if you've planned properly) or to rebalance your portfolio each year to bring it back in line with your targeted asset allocation.

Enemy #6 – Life Unexpected

Life happens, and, when it does, it sometimes has a tendency to get in the way of the things we are trying do for ourselves and our families. The one certainty on which we can count is that life is full of uncertainty, so why aren't we more prepared? Most people are just a paycheck away from financial disaster, yet the odds of an unexpected occurrence such as a job loss, a medical emergency, a devastating accident, or even a death in the family are fairly high when you consider them all together. Taken as whole, the question is not if a financial disaster will strike, but when.

The issue really comes down to individual responsibility and common sense foresight. Stuff happens when it is least expected and it is up to the individual to guard against possible financial consequences. Here are five essential steps everyone needs to take to prepare for the unexpected:

Establish an emergency fund

Everyone should have enough money set aside in a short term savings account to cover six to twelve months' worth of living expenses.

Insure everything

If you own it, you should insure it: Everything, from your home, your car to all of the possession inside both. If you rent, you can still insure your possessions.

Insure your health

If you don't have employer provided health insurance, you need to purchase your own. If you think you're young and invincible, stop it, and buy high deductible coverage for major medical expenses. You can also contribute to a tax deductible Health Saving Account to help pay your deductible.

Insure your biggest risk

Before you turn 65 you have a one in five chance of suffering a long term disability that will prevent you from working for more than 90 days. If your employer doesn't offer long term disability, then you should look into some individual coverage. Not everyone can qualify for it, so if you do, then you should buy it.

Insure your life

If you have someone who is dependent upon you for their financial security, then it is an absolute no brainer. Not only is buying life insurance to protect family members a demonstration of unconditional love, it is just the responsible thing to do.

Enemy # 7 – Lawsuits

There is just no way around it; we live in a hyper-litigious society, with people ready to sue at the drop of a hat. From someone stubbing their toe on a crack in the sidewalk outside your house, to the person who didn't like what you had to say about him to his colleagues – there are people on the constant lookout for deep pockets. The big mistake most people make is to assume their exposure to liability claims is covered by their homeowner's insurance. Considering that medical bills could run into the hundreds of thousands, the typical $300,000 liability cap in homeowner's insurance policies would leave most people exposed. Any judgment in excess of that would target your assets and, possibly your wages. Anyone with any amount of assets to protect should buy a Personal Umbrella Liability insurance policy. At an average premium rate of $300 per $1 million of coverage, it is the best deal in insurance coverage.

Enemy # 8 – Unintended Heirs

We spend a lifetime creating assets that we would eventually like to pass on to our children and their children. However, we all live under the threat of a legal system which doesn't necessarily share your intent, and if you don't do it for yourself, the state will plan your estate for you. By default, the state will decide how and to whom you assets are distributed; it will choose a guardian for your children; and it can make financial and health decision on your behalf when you are unable due to incapacitation or death. Your estate plan must incorporate legal protections that will ensure that your expectations and intentions control the decisions made on your behalf. At a minimum, it should include a will, a power of attorney, a living will or health care proxy, and a living trust.

For larger estates of $5 million or more, the federal government could become your largest unintended heir. If your estate is left unprotected, without the proper mechanisms in place to shield it, the IRS could take as much as 40 percent of your assets to cover your estate tax bill. For the cost of a short family vacation, you can work with an estate planning professional, preferably an estate attorney in combination with a financial advisor experienced in estate planning, to implement strategies that can minimize your estate taxes in order to maximize your estate for your intended heirs.

Conclusion

Of the hundreds of decisions we make each day, those having to do with our finances are among the most frequent and consequential. And, aside from, perhaps, decisions we make concerning our relationships, the decisions we make dealing with any aspect of our finances are the most emotionally charged. That's not to say that emotions in decision-making are necessarily bad – instincts can prove to be valuable in some instances – however, they can tend to skew our decision-making ability. The more powerful emotions – fear, greed, insecurity, self-doubt, sadness – can overwhelm our perception of available options or solutions often narrowing them to the ones that cater to our emotional state at the moment. Hence, unless we are aware of our emotions and which ones happen to occupy our state of mind when a decision is required, we stand a much higher chance of making a bad decision.

When we know ourselves (through the financial planning process) and we can identify the threats to our wealth, our choices become clearer and our financial decisions are guided by definitive strategies designed to meet our specific objectives while neutralizing the threat. By focusing strictly on our financial objectives and our potential obstacles, we can more easily detach ourselves from those emotions that can lead to financial inertia or regretful decisions.

Chapter Exercise

- List your most important financial goals (i.e. retirement, a home purchase, a college education for your children, etc.). Be specific with target dates and how much you would expect to your goals to cost.
- If you haven't already, take an hour to develop a realistic budget that incorporates your financial goals and spending priorities. The budget worksheet included at the end of this chapter is an excellent starting point. Build the critical habit of monitoring your spending each day.
- List your most important financial goals. For each, identify the threats to achieving them. Then list one action step you can take immediately to eliminate the threat. For example:

Systems to implement as a habit
when applicable to your situation:

I. Developing a personal cash flow management system:

1. Prepare a Budget-Extremely essential to managing finances. Use apps like Mint or just write it on paper or use excel.

2. Through the workshop discover the hidden techniques of putting your cash flow on auto-pilot in your lifestyle, planning, and wage account.

3. Through the workshop uncover the commitments you need to make each month from each account and set it on auto-pilot.

Take the management out of the cash flow with The Auto-Pilot Cash Flow System™ at http://www.BizActionCoach.com/product/the-auto-pilot-cash-flow-management/

II. The Debt Management System:

1. Through the workshop discover the hidden ways to structure your liquidity ratio in your assets to prevent from debt disaster.

2. Discover the hidden secret of dividing your debt and structuring your payments to paying off your debt sooner than you expect.

3. Put the system on auto-pilot combined with strategies to make changes along the way.

Reduce or eliminate debt with The Debt-Management System™ workshop at http://www.BizActionCoach.com/product/the-debt-management-system/

III. The Tax-Diversification Strategy for Retirement:

1. Write down your retirement income goal.

2. Through the workshop discover an easy and realistic way to accurately assess your income requirements throughout your retirement.
3. Find out hidden ways to get the essential part of the income on a tax-free basis

Retire peacefully with The Retirement Diversification Strategy™ workshop at http://www.BizActionCoach.com/product/the-retirement-diversification/

V. The Estate Diversification Strategy:
1. Divide the current value of all your assets in three buckets – Tax Now, Tax Later, and Tax Free.
2. Discover the hidden techniques of how to accurately assess the growth of your estate and not random unrealistic growth rates.
3. With the help of the workshop, find the amount of assets you need to maintain in the tax–free bucket to take care of the taxes that will be due in the other buckets.

Pass on your legacy with The Estate Diversification Strategy™ workshop at http://www.BizActionCoach.com/product/the-estate-diversification/

VI. Preparing for the Unexpected:
1. Through the workshop, discover what insurances you need and what you don't.

2. Find out the hidden strategies that help you pay the least out of pocket for insurances.

3. Put a deadline as to who will implement what by when to achieve the result.

Be prepared for the unexpected with The Unexpected Preparation™ http://www.BizActionCoach.com/product/the-unexpected-preparation/

VII. Building Financial Behavior Discipline:

1. Through the workshop, discover the secret behind making successful major financial decisions and how to convert those into habits.

2. Find out hidden ways to change your habits and follow that routine for 21 days.

3. Compare the decisions you make on larger investments or macro decisions now compared to what you did before. You will notice a difference.

Build an everlasting effective financial behavior The Essential Financial Behavior Discipline™ at http://www.BizActionCoach.com/product/the-essential-financial-behavior/

Get the entire deck of cards (52 Cards-52 Systems) at http://www.BizActionCoach.com/product/the-deck-of-cards-workshop-system/

Retire by age 65

Threat	Action Step
Not saving enough	Create a budget and reduce non-essential expenses
Low return on investment	Consult with a financial advisor on how to improve returns without taking on too much risk
Too much debt	Create a budget and debt payoff plan
Not sure how much I will need to save	Consult with a financial advisor to determine how much I will need

Then, take action today!

{Note: With many independent financial advisors there is no cost or obligation for a consultation.}

Please complete the exercise on the next page before proceeding to read the next chapter:

What thought or thoughts come to your mind after reading this chapter?

_____

_____

_____

_____

_____

_____

_____

What Decision or Decisions have you made about the thought or thoughts you had?

_____

_____

_____

_____

_____

_____

_____

What Growth Actions would you take today or by a specific date to implement your thoughts?

_____

_____

_____

_____

_____

_____

_____

A True Story

I have been a true follower of protecting and securing myself from enemies of wealth. I have never lost wealth during the two market crashes I went through and I have always held on to all my real estate holdings. They have paid off well. I have always protected myself from unexpected events by carrying the appropriate insurance and had my estate planning constantly updated whenever needed. So I talk the talk and walk the walk.

Chapter 6

simplifying critical business decisions

for most entrepreneurs, launching a business can be both exhilarating and terrifying – like a roller coaster ride that takes you careening from highs to lows and whipping you side-to-side as you hold on for dear life. The difference is that roller coaster rides are predictable and always end smoothly and softly. A new and growing business is far less predictable and the end can come abruptly if bad choices are made along the way. Building a business requires taking risks, overcoming obstacles, and, most daunting of all, making dozens of consequential decisions every day. Each decision can have a ripple effect that stretches far and wide, for better or worse. Quite simply, success or failure becomes a function of the number of good decisions versus bad decisions a business owner makes.

Of course, it's never quite as simple as this, but if we could clearly identify the traits of unsuccessful and successful business owners, we might just find the unsuccessful owners operating within the Bad 5 C's of Life (Chaos, Confusion, Conflict, Complaints, and Clutter – see Chapter Three) while successful owners operate in the world of the Good 5 C's of Life (Clarity, Confidence, Creativity, Critical Thinking and Conviction). Business owners who lack clarity of purpose and operate within chaos will wallow in ambiguity and intuition, while those who have a clear vision of and a sense of purpose, can more often decide with clarity and confidence.

Failing businesses tend to be led by owners who, for fear of making a bad decision, will retreat into the comfort of indecision which can be more destructive than making a bad decision. At least with a bad decision, you can measure the outcome against the intent of the decision, adjust and try again. That's how you turn failure into success. With indecision, there is nothing to measure other than the status quo. In most cases, the risk of a bad decision is far less painful than the lingering doubt and dread of indecision.

As with everyday personal decisions, the key to making better business decisions is to be able to elevate your objectivity while compartmentalizing your biases. The Decision Simplifier™ tool, as explained in Chapter 2, enables you to focus quickly on those factors on either side of the equation which will influence the outcome. The decision becomes clear when the results of the Decision Simplifier™

process weigh more heavily on the side of "Do It" or "Don't Do It."

It really doesn't have to be more complicated than that, unless, of course, you are still struggling in the world of the Bad 5 C's of Life, dominated by Chaos, Confusion, Conflict, Complaints, and Clutter. Until you have worked your way into the world of the Good 5 C's of Life, where Clarity, Confidence, Creativity, Critical Thinking and Conviction rule your perspective, even a decision-making process as simple as the Decision Simplifier can be challenging.

Although volumes have been written on the subject and MBA schools build whole curriculums around it, today's business experts have come to agree on five key imperatives that will drive your business success:

I. You must have a plan
II. You must know what you don't know
III. You must master cash flow management
IV. You must develop your Unique Ability® and differentiate
V. You must Narrow Your Focus

Should you make these imperatives your sole focus, the unyielding basis for running your business, and the primary measure of your progress, the by-product of your efforts will be a dramatic boost in the power of your decisiveness.

You must have a Business Plan

Launching any business without a business plan is like trying to steer a boat without a rudder; although you're moving, you're moving in no particular direction and you're likely to end up anywhere but where you hoped to be. And, for business owners, hope is not a strategy. Also consider that, if you are ever in a position to need money – a capital infusion through a bank loan, an investor or a partner – without a business plan you'll have a difficult time convincing others that your business has clear path to success.

A well-conceived, detailed business plan is the strategic document that forms the basis of most of your business decisions; so, in essence, it is a decision simplifier tool. First and foremost, it enables you to really understand your business especially in the context of your industry, the marketplace, your competition and your customers. Then, as you become aware of the complexities of your business, you become more informed of the practices and processes that have the highest probability of success.

Where the tire hits the road, your business plan is your guide for communicating your vision to your employees, customers and investors which is critical to the growth of your business. In terms of the day-to-day management of your business, your plan sets and prioritizes your strategies and determines the what, how and when of allocating resources, essentially facilitating informed decision-making. Equally important, your plan becomes the benchmark against which progress can be measured and calculated adjustments made to keep you on course.

Developing a business plan isn't rocket science, and it shouldn't require a one-inch binder to contain it; however, it must include some key elements that require careful thought and realistic forecasting. A well-conceived business plan could be presented on no more than five or six pages; more if you want to include the details of any research. At a minimum your business plan should include:

An Executive Summary

This is a half to one-page synopsis of your overall plan. Should you ever need to present your business plan to a banker or a potential investor or partner; the summary should state your intention of raising capital along with its purpose.

You have to write your own business plan and do not outsource it. It is your business and only you know your unique strengths and somebody else cannot visualize it for you. So when you write the executive summary, it should focus on the big WHY and why you do what you do and how it can benefit the world. You also have to stress why your services or product is essential. You have to summarize how you plan to capture customers, what is process for converting those into real customers, and how those customers will be committed to doing more things with you or buying more things.

Market Analysis

This is where you demonstrate to your readers and yourself your knowledge about your industry. The market analysis defines your target market in terms of size, growth potential, trends and sales potential. Your market analysis also forms the basis for your pricing as well as for determining marketing and distribution methods.

Apple thrives because it has captured 70 percent of a niche target market. They only targeted 7 percent of the market, but they dominate that 7 percent by capturing 70 percent of that market. So what is your target market? How narrow and specific it is? What are the demographics, psychographics, and lifestyle habits of these customers? How will your product or service fit their lifestyle? Most importantly, why should they buy your product or service?

Business Description

This is the why, what and how explanation of your business purpose. Your business description provides an overview of your business purpose, the different elements that comprise your business, and the critical factors that will drive its success.

This is where you have to focus on how the business can be run without you. Is it or can it become a self-managing company? Will the business provide decent owner compensation and build enough profits for it to continue its growth? A business only has value, when there is decent owner compensation and there is potential for growth. Amazon and some of the other companies are exceptions to this, but in general, you want to strive to achieve good owner compensation and profit.

Business Structure and Management

This describes how you are organized as a business, including ownership, bios of your management team, and particular qualifications of your board members or expert consultants.

Your business structure needs to be clear and distinct. It should have a unique process and show how a customer is acquired and who is responsible for what to the point that customer is committed to continuing to do business with you and provide referrals of new customers. It is very important that you do not out source any of this to anyone and write it yourself. Any business plan written by someone else is not yours and is just a bunch of papers with text and visuals for a fee. This is a livelihood you have to make and you have to figure out yourself how to do the same.

Marketing and Sales Strategies

This is the heart of your plan which describes how you create the lifeblood of your business – a constant stream of customers and repeat business. It must clearly define the strategies and tactics you will use to market to your potential customers and the sales process you'll use to reel them in.

The marketing and sales process should be focused on three aspects:

a. Lead Generation: How do you generate leads? What is the cost? How you are going to make it successful? How reliable it is to use it on an ongoing basis?

b. Lead Conversion: How do you convert the leads you have into customers? How will they stay committed during the whole journey? How will they buy more stuff or do more business with you?

c. Lead Creation: How will the customers you have create new leads for you? Why will they create new leads for you? What are alternates if one strategy fails? Alternates are very important and it is very important that for every objective you want to achieve, you have plan A through plan D in case one fails. Failure is inevitable. Be prepared for it and have the courage to fail even more.

Product or Service Description

Here you describe what it is exactly that you are offering. It should be relatively short on technical details and longer on the benefits your customers will derive from using the product or service. It's important to emphasize your unique value proposition – the value your clients will receive that they couldn't receive from any of your competitors.

Your product description is where you have to show how you intend to dominate the market and outshine your competition. If you think you have no competition, you have not described your product or service very well. Every business has competition and every successful business just finds ways to outsmart the competition. What are your ways that you will outsmart your competitors?

Capital Needs

If you are looking for capital, this is where you indicate the amount you are looking for, how it will be used and the returns you expect from its use.

Whenever you present capital needs, it is very essential you breakdown how the capital will be used in each area and what you expect the ideal outcome to be for each element within each area. You have to know the best case scenario and worst case scenario of the use of the capital for each element within each area to understand the risk and ROI (return on investment). Without these details, every venture capital investor or angel investor or bank may not be willing to give you what you want. Every person who is willing to give you money wants to know what you are going to do with their funds, how much risk they have, what return they can expect, and most importantly how much do you believe in what you are selling. Without that belief and conviction, everything else is meaningless.

Financial Statement and Cash Flow Projection

If you've been in business for a while, this should include three to five years of historical data. For established businesses as well as start-ups, it should include cash flow projections that reflect your market analysis and state objectives.

You have to be very realistic in your cash flow projections. A vague projection of cash flow throws off any business plan out the window, no matter how well it is written. The revenue projection should be broken down as to how much you expect from each source and how you came to that conclusion. If that is believable, you have the investors or bank's attention. Next, you have to show how frugal are you with your expenses and what proof you have that shows you can keep the expenses that low. You have to "show the proof, tell the truth, and obey the law."

All the expenses you project are legit and you are not trying to skim more money from bank or investor for personal benefit.

Although, a good business plan does establish a clear purpose and objectives, it's not uncommon for the strategies and tactics to evolve as your business and knowledge of the industry evolves. It is important to review your business plan at least once per quarter to gauge results, make adjustments, and update your analysis based on new trends, technologies, or competition.

Above all, you should not try to go it alone. Even if you are a sole proprietor, you need someone to whom you can be accountable to see that the plan is properly developed, implemented and monitored. Even start-up business owners can form an advisory board consisting of colleagues, family members, mentors, and business leaders. They become a critical sounding board and a source of valuable advice when key decisions have to be made.

You Must Know What You Don't Know

"The world belongs to the people who ask great questions, not to the ones who have all the answers."
—Bimal Shah

When running a business, hindsight is definitely 20/20, and, it's often possible to use hindsight to change the outcome if given a second opportunity. Well before any decision turns into action, a business owner can gain much of the hindsight they need by asking the right questions. Business owners can't be responsible for having all of the answers they need to successfully run a business; however, they do need to take responsibility for knowing what they don't know and asking enough questions to obtain the answers.

To gain better understanding for this most fundamental law of wisdom, take a moment to consider the following parable:

The Ripple Effect:

 The Master was walking through the fields one day when a young man with a troubled look on his face approached him. "On such a beautiful day, it must be difficult to stay so serious," the Master said.

 "Is it? I hadn't noticed," the young man said, turning to look around and notice his surroundings. His eyes scanned the landscape, but nothing seemed to register, his mind was elsewhere.

 Watching intently, the Master continued to walk. "Join me if you like." The Master walked to the edge of a still pond framed by sycamore trees, their leaves golden orange and about to fall.

 "Please sit down." the Master instructed. Straining his eyes to not miss a single detail, the man looked at the water's surface. "I see ripples." "Where did the ripples come from?"

 "From the pebble I threw in the pond, Master."

 "Please reach your hand into the water and stop the ripples," the Master directed. Not understanding, the young man stuck his hand in the water as a ripple neared, only to cause more ripples.

 The young man was now completely baffled. Where was this going? Had he made a mistake in seeking out the Master?

After all, he was not a student. Perhaps he could not be helped. Puzzled, the young man waited.

"Were you able to stop the ripples with your hands?" the Master asked.

"No, of course not," came the frustrated reply.

"Could you have stopped the ripples, then?"

"No Master. I told you I only caused more ripples."

"What is if you had stopped the pebble from entering the water to begin with?" The Master smiled such a beautiful smile; the young man could not be upset. "Next time you are unhappy with your life, catch the stone before it hits the water. Do not spend time trying to undo what you have done. Rather, change what you are going to do before you do it." The Master looked kindly upon the young man.

"But Master, how will I know what I am going to do before I do it?"

"Take the responsibility for living your own life. If you're working with a doctor to treat an illness, ask the doctor to help you understand what caused the illness. Do not just treat the ripple. Keep asking questions."

The young man stopped, his mind reeling. "But I came to you ask you for answers. Are you saying that I know the answers?"

"You may not have the answers right now, but if you ask the right questions, then you shall discover the answers."

But what are the right questions, Master?"

"There are no wrong questions, only unasked ones. We must ask, for, without asking, we cannot receive answers. But it is your responsibility to ask. No one else can do that for you."

When a stone is dropped in a pond, it creates a series of concentric ripples that expand over the surface of the water, disrupting everything in their path. In the business world, the ripple effect is the notion that a single action can affect aspects of a business far removed from its intended purpose, with unpredictable consequences. Although no one can possibly predict all of the consequences of an action ahead of time, the outcome can be more controllable when questions are answered in advance.

It's been said that the "key to wisdom is in knowing all the right questions." In searching for life's answers, the young man in the parable will be far better off, even if he has to ask many wrong questions in order to find the right one. However, business owners often don't have the advantage of time to find the right questions.

Beware the "IKEA" Syndrome

In my interactions with business owners, I have too often observed instances of the IKEA Syndrome – "I Know Everything Already" – a potentially fatal condition that ignores the fact that information in the digital world is doubling every two years. That would imply that, just to keep pace, to keep from falling behind, we humans must be able to double our knowledge every two years. In an ultra-competitive environment where knowledge is power and relevance can be fleeting, that could spell doom for any business.

Business owners who suffer from the IKEA syndrome tend to dwell in the present (or even the past), giving little thought to the changing world around them. The most successful businesses devote much of their energy to anticipating the future, to innovating in order to remain relevant. Highly successful entrepreneurs like Bill Gates and Steve Jobs may come across as "know-it-alls;" however, the true key to their success was their resistance to the status quo and their thirst for knowledge. They not only anticipated the future; in many respects, they created it – but only after learning more about what they did not already know.

In order to avoid the IKEA Syndrome, a business owner must recognize that, business people like Gates, Jobs and anyone else who is at the pinnacle of business recognize the fundamental principle of business, which is if you're not constantly striving to improve, you'll always be falling behind. That's because we never stay the same – we're either getting better or getting worse; and if everyone else is striving to get better, by doing nothing, you are actually getting worse. To ensure constant business growth, business owners must become overly curious lifetime learners in their craft as well as the world around them.

Business owners need to engage in learning at every opportunity, including:

- Attending industry trade conferences and events
- Subscribe to RSS feeds from industry related websites
- Network with other business owners to glean new ideas
- Learn about one new technological innovation each month
- Read a good book that inspires (try reading at least 10 pages each day)

- Surround yourself with positive, forward thinking people
- Take a personal development course such as Dale Carnegie
- Get under the wing of a mentor or coach who can inspire you to learn new things

You must Master Cash Flow Management

Most entrepreneurs rely on their core competency to launch an idea and turn it into profitable business; and, that core competency is typically centered on creating a product or service people will want to buy and then getting it out the door. Entrepreneurs generally don't go into business to be able to manage the books. Yet most small business owners cite as their number one concern lack of cash flow, and with good reason. According to Dunn and Bradstreet, 96 percent of businesses fail due to managerial incompetence; and of those, 82 percent fail due to poor cash flow management skills or a poor understanding of cash flow.

It's not just declining sales or poor economic conditions that lead to cash flow problems. Talk with any business expert and they will tell you stories of businesses that were very profitable but grew themselves into trouble when their cash couldn't keep pace with their increasing expenses. Or, they were highly profitable but they allowed their accounts receivable to get out of control. Those are particularly tragic ways for a business to die.

Simplifying Cash Flow Management Decisions

In Chapter 5 we discussed the notion of managing your personal cash flow like a successful business, using a three-bucket strategy that resembles the cash flow allocation a company might employ. For individuals and businesses alike, the goal is the same – to simplify, and to the greatest extent possible, automate. Breaking cash flow management decision down to smaller, more manageable pieces or buckets, each with clearly defined objectives or purposes, takes "decision-making" out of the equation.

Three Bucket Strategy for Cash Flow Management

As with the personal three bucket strategy, the business equivalent requires establishing three separate accounts with specific guidelines for managing them:

A. Operations Account: In this account you would maintain a daily balance of your operational expenses and add a ten to twenty percent buffer for any cost increases that you may see happening based on the industry or type of business you are in. Operational expenses are expenses that you need to spend to normally run your business. These are not expansion or growth related expenses.

What Goes In and Out: The Monthly Set amount required for operations of the business at the current revenue level. As your revenue level changes, your operations account changes accordingly. The level that you maintain in your operations account can also change from time to time based on the growth of your business.

B. Growth Account: This is the account where you leave funds available for expansion, capital expenditures, employee expansion and in general expenditures that you want to allocate for growth of your business. It could be for the launch of a major marketing campaign, a new product launch, the expansion of your facility, or anything in your strategic plan earmarked for growth.

What Goes In and Out: Anything in excess of the Operations account set amount & Reserve account required balance goes in. What goes out is all growth related expenses for the business.

C. Reserve Account: This is the equivalent of an emergency account, in which you would maintain at least six months of monthly operations amount as a balance if you have no debt. If you have business debt, at least 15 percent of your outstanding debt amount to a recommended amount of 25 percent of your outstanding business debt amount should be maintained.

Utilizing this simple three bucket strategy should go a long way to keeping you out of cash flow trouble.

You Must Develop Your Unique Ability and Differentiate

A few years ago, I had the very good fortune of being introduced to Dan Sullivan, a true innovator in the realm of entrepreneurial development. Over several decades he has established himself as the foremost coach to highly successful business people, helping them to realize their full potential in both their personal and business lives. I enrolled in Dan's Strategic Coach® program, which has successfully produced life-changing breakthroughs for thousands of business people and entrepreneurs. The central tenet of Dan's teachings and the core of his Strategic Coaching program is a concept he has termed, *The Unique Ability*®, which, when fully embraced, can unleash the potential in anyone seeking to overcome the gravitational forces that keep them from achieving total fulfillment in both their business and their personal lives.

At its core, The Unique Ability® recognizes that there is an incredible force within each of us consisting of our talents, passions and skills that have yet to be utilized. When harnessed and focused, they become a superior ability that can differentiate us in a way that people recognize and value. More important, it's an ability about which we are so passionate that we seek to find ways to exercise it as much as possible, and find ways to improve it. When this happens, it not only energizes us, it energizes the people around us, including our employees and our customers. The ultimate challenge for any person is to find it, develop it and, to maximum extent possible fulfill it; and when you do, it can transform your life such that happiness is all that you will know.

That's a remarkable claim; but, if you think about it, it would have to be true. After all, if you are able to spend all of your time doing what you love to do while making a difference in the lives of others, how could that not bring you ultimate fulfillment? Discovering and developing your Unique Ability defines your purpose in life, and, as we have discussed extensively in this book, purpose is one of the keys to happiness.

Consider this – when you are able to harness your energies – physical, mental and emotional – around the things you love doing, you have no real obstacles other than trying to optimize the time you can spend doing it. It actually forces you to learn how to delegate the things that keep you from working on your Unique Ability. Taking this concept further, you can find or hire people who love doing what you have to delegate. It also forces you to look at ways to automate those aspects of your business that might otherwise require your time and attention to manage them.

When you allow yourself to focus strictly on your Unique Ability, you don't have to limit yourself to just becoming competent or even excellent. Competence is simply the bare minimum ability in order to do what might be expected of us; and excellence, while commendable and certainly more desirable, is simply the standard by which all businesses are measured today. You can't exist in the marketplace without striving for excellence; but excellence without true passion is merely skills performed with the greatest amount of proficiency.

To truly differentiate yourself and your business, to have any chance of separating your brand from the rest, is to be exceptional. To be exceptional means to always be performing your Unique Ability, your superior skill with passion. That's when people – your customers, your employees, even your competition – will take notice. That's when you can reach the pinnacle.

Obviously, I recommend Dan's book, *Unique Ability®: Creating the Life You Want,* to anyone who wants to discover and develop their Unique Ability and transform their lives. But, for entrepreneurs, especially those who want to truly make a difference and who want to truly differentiate themselves, it is essential reading.

You Must Choose Your Customers, Narrow Your Focus and Dominate Your Market

The title of this section actually comes from the title of great book that I commend to anyone with aspirations of achieving uncommon success in their business. The book is, *The Discipline of Market Leaders: Choose Your Customers, Narrow Your Focus and Dominate Your Market*, by Michael Treacy and Fred Wiersema. It was written more than two decades ago so it might be slightly outdated, but its premise is as valid today, if not more so, than it was then; and that is that successful businesses – those which become the market leaders – are exceptional at delivering one type of value to their chosen customers. By focusing their energy and resources on a single discipline, and increasing its value to their customers year after year, they can remain exceptional in the eyes of their customers, which will ensure sustained growth and profitability.

The book focuses on three value disciplines that all businesses must be able to master; but they must choose one at which to become exceptional:

Product Innovation: Be able to keep their products relevant, if not cutting edge, in a dynamic and evolving marketplace. Think Apple.

Operational Excellence: Offer the lowest prices in the most convenient way. Think Amazon.

Customer Intimacy: Offer tailored customer-focused solutions that meet the specific needs of a targeted group of customers. Think Nordstrom.

So, the question becomes which value discipline should your business pursue? The fundamental premise of the book is that, if you try to pursue all three, you will risk being exceptional at none which will render you to the lower tier of your market. Of course, to some extent you have to pursue all three in order to exist in the market. But there has to be just one on which you will stake your brand and your future, around which you will organize your business, focus your energy and resources, and build your culture.

Becoming exceptional at any one of the three value disciplines will lead to the same outcome expected by market leaders – to create stark raving fans out of your customers. Think of any market leader and you can usually identify what it is that they do better than anyone else. There is a unique value they provide that sets them apart from the competition. And, they constantly strive to increase that value year after year.

By choosing your customers and narrowing your focus, your business will be better positioned to overcome the common mistakes made by many businesses that prevent them from becoming market leaders:

Not having a clearly defined "ideal" customer

When starting a business, there is a great temptation to try to be all things to all people and cater to any warm body in order to create as much opportunity for customer growth as possible. In reality, this strategy can have the opposite effect and prevent the business from establishing a true growth pattern. First, it almost guarantees inefficiency as energy and resources are spread across less productive or profitable business lines. Second, it perpetuates business-wide mediocrity as the opportunity to excel in any market segment is diluted by inefficiency. Third, and most important, the customers you really want to attract won't see how your business offers any unique value that warrants their patronage.

You must choose your ideal customer and narrow your focus to offer uncommon value even if it means gaining one customer at a time. Done right, you will create one stark raving fan at a time which will quickly blossom into a base of ideal customers.

Not having a clear and concise message

The old adage, "You don't get a second chance to make a first impression," is no truer than for a business trying to establish itself in a particular market much less trying to become a market leader. If you can't answer the one question on the mind of any potential customer – "Why should I do business with you when there are dozens of other companies offering the same product or service? – In a concise and compelling way, it probably means you don't clearly understand your target buyer. These three key issues go to the heart of a value proposition which is very brief (one to two sentences) summary of the most persuasive reasons people should notice you and answer your call to action.

Quite simply, people won't buy from you if they don't understand why they should even consider you; and, whether it's a single sentence at the top of your website's home page, or from your lips as you ride an elevator with a potential customer, if you can't clearly describe the promise of value you can deliver you will lose opportunities.

When you truly know your customer and the problems they want to solve, and you've narrowed your focus to the value discipline that you deliver better than anyone else, your value proposition practically creates itself.

Not really and deeply connecting with to your customers

When you consider the market leaders of today, they may offer the best product, the least cost, the best customer experience; but any of those advantages may only be fleeting as competitors rise up with better alternatives. The true market leaders, the ones that enduringly dominate their markets, offer something that most of their competitors can't match – a real and deep connection with their customers. Even if you have clearly defined your target customer and have crafted the clearest and most compelling value proposition to attract them, if you fail to find ways to increase the value of your relationship with them, they will eventually slip away.

The most successful companies make customer loyalty their number one priority. Why? Because companies generate the greatest profit when they can increase the Lifetime Value of a Customer – through repeat sales and referrals. Otherwise, a business must spend most of its time, energy and resources acquiring new customers which is the least profitable activity.

You need to know your customer and narrow your focus to a value discipline that not only differentiates you in the marketplace, it must be constantly refined, improved and communicated so your customer knows you know them.

Systems to implement as a habit when applicable to your situation:

I. Developing your "Why"– A purpose for the business:

1. Discover the hidden ways to uncover your why – why you do what you do.

2. Find the secret on how to sharpen your why to differentiate yourself from the competition and make you a dominator, not a competitor.

3. Through the workshop, discover your short succinct why that appeals to your target market or audience. (For Example – Chase is in business, so people can Chase what matters. FedEx is in business so the World is On Time to get things done.

Discover the system to develop your WHY The "Why" Developer™ at http://www.BizActionCoach.com/product/the-why-developer/

II. The Business Cash Flow System:

1. Through the workshop discover the secret ways to avoid cash flow disasters in your business and put your systems in auto-pilot.

2. Find the hidden ways to auto-pilot the right cash flow in each of the three accounts – The Operations, The Growth Account, and The Reserve.
3. Set up auto-deposit into each account to the amount as determined by the exercise in the workshop
4. Through the exercise, determine strategies you need to layout for adjustments and changes along the way.

Automate Business Cash Flow with The Business Cash Flow Management System™ workshop at http://www.BizActionCoach.com/product/the-business-cash-flow-management-system/

III. Differentiating yourself from the competition:
1. Identify 10 weak points in your competition.
2. Through the workshop, discover hidden ways to overcome your weak points and your competitors weak points
3. With the workshop, discover secret strategies that can make attracting your customers very easy and how to dramatically reduce your customer acquisition cost.

Stand out from our competition with The Business Differentiation™ workshop at http://www.BizActionCoach.com/product/the-business-differentiation/

IV. Deeply connecting to your customers in every message that goes out:

1. Through the workshop, discover the hidden ways to get people interested in your message
2. Unearth the secret strategies that emotionally and intellectually get the customer connected.
3. Build the commitment and call to action in your message and measure your responses.

Build a strong message with The Connected Customer™ workshop at http://www.BizActionCoach.com/product/the-connected-customer/

V. Calculating Your Most Valuable Hourly Pay

1. Through the workshop, discover the biggest mistakes entrepreneurs make when calculating their hourly pay.
2. Through the exercise in the workshop, find hidden ways of calculating your true hourly pay of where it should be and where it truly is.
3. Develop list of activities that are aligned with your true hourly pay of where it should be to start making more money and start implementing the same.

Increase your business revenues with The Entrepreneur's Pay™ at http://www.BizActionCoach.com/product/the-entrepreneurs-pay/

VI. Narrowing your customer base:

1. List your top 5 customers that did the most business in the past 12 months and the top 5 customers over the last 5 years.

2. Through the workshop, discover the hidden ways to leverage and capitalize on the opportunities you have, will have, your capabilities and your resources.

3. With the aid of the workshop, build a list of steps and determine who needs to do them by when.

Narrow your customer focus with The Customer Base Focuser™ http://www.BizActionCoach.com/product/the-customer-base-focuser/

Get the entire deck of cards (52 Cards-52 Systems) at http://www.BizActionCoach.com/product/the-deck-of-cards-workshop-system/

Chapter Workbook

- **Build your business plan.** If you don't have a business plan, stop what you are doing and build one. You won't have a real business until you do. You can go online and download a software program that will practically build it for you. There are many to choose from, however, for $99, Business Plan Pro (businessplanpro.com) is a robust planning tool ideal for beginners.

- **Build an advisory panel.** No business owner should try to go it alone. You need people who are on your side who are genuinely interested in your success.

An advisory panel consisting of mentors, business colleagues, community leaders, and professional advisors can provide invaluable support in terms of accountability, feedback, and guidance.

- **Make a commitment to learn one new thing about your business, your market, technology or yourself each week.** Force yourself to expand your knowledge and self-awareness. You can start by buying Dan Sullivan's book, *Unique Ability®: Creating the Life You Want.*

- **Develop your Unique Ability.** Identify what it is that you are passionate about – in business or your personal life – and create a plan to develop it, nurture it and, if it can be done, monetize it so that you can make your living do what you love.

- **Take an online business course on cash flow management for entrepreneurs.** You don't plan on being your business' CFO forever; but until you can delegate it, you need to master it.

- **Decide who your ideal customer is and then determine which value discipline you can focus on to create uncommon value for him.** Revisit your business plan to restructure your business blueprint accordingly.

- **Refine your message.** If your value proposition doesn't clearly target your ideal customer and communicate your unique value in two sentences or less, it needs work.

Please complete the exercise on the next page before proceeding to read the next chapter.

What thought or thoughts come to your mind after reading this chapter?

_____

_____

_____

_____

_____

_____

_____

What Decision or Decisions have you made about the thought or thoughts you had?

_____

_____

_____

_____

_____

_____

_____

What Growth Actions would you take today or by a specific date to implement your thoughts?

_____

_____

_____

_____

_____

_____

_____

A True Story

I have been in business for 17 years and I have grown by saying no to tasks that I shouldn't do and no to people that I cannot serve or cannot have as customers. It is very important that we say no to tasks that we don't need to do and no to customers that are not a good fit for us. We all have a "To Do" list and early on in my professional career I started preparing a "Not to Do" list. I still today maintain the habit of having a "not to do list" and constantly update it as and when needed.

Chapter 7

the 80/20 principle
for happiness

f or many of us, the failure to achieve happiness or
fulfillment is often attributed to the constraints of
time placed on us by our demanding lives – so much
to do and so little time. How often have you heard yourself,
or anyone else says "If there was just one more hour in the
day;" as if that one additional hour could somehow make a
significant difference in what you could accomplish. What
would you do with that hour? How would you spend a
gift of an hour that would make an appreciable difference
in your life? Or, would you use it in the same way you
spend the rest of your time within the constraint of a
24-hour day?

The fact of the matter is that we can't change the number of hours in the day; however, we can change what we do with the time we are given. Consider that, on average, people spend just 20 percent of their time on activities that produce any positive outcomes in their life – strengthening relationships, improving the life of others, improving their health and wellness, working towards goals, or self-development. The other 80 percent is spent on activity, or non-activity, that does little or nothing to advance the ball in the game of life – paper pushing, internet surfing, worrying, sitting in traffic, gossiping, watching TV, mindlessly eating, thinking about what you should be doing, along with the hundreds of other things people can find to do to spend 80 percent of their time.

Now consider the inverse of that equation. If, on average, 20 percent of our activity is responsible for 80 percent of the positive outcomes we experience, what could we gain by increasing the amount of time spent in that activity? If, say, we were able to spend 30 percent of our time in purposeful, planned activity, wouldn't we expand our capacity to enjoy greater fulfillment and more positive outcomes? By increasing that percentage incrementally, isn't possible to eventually lead a life in which the vast majority of our time is spent doing the things that can bring happiness?

Of course, there is no real way to quantify this theory; however, simple common sense prevails. The more time we can spend doing the things that we enjoy or that can actually improve our lot in life, the happier we can be. It seems simple and clear; however, if it were, why then are we constantly barraged with statistics like the following – each one an indication of the little amount of time people are spending trying to create positive outcomes in their lives:

- According to the American Dental Association, 155.9 Million People do not floss daily.
- According to CDC in 2013, 80 percent of American Adult Population doesn't get the recommended exercise; also, 69 percent of the population age 20 and older is overweight.
- 50 million Americans eat fast food each day.
- According to Gallup in their State of the American Workplace report, 70 percent of workers are not actively engaged or are disengaged at work, which costs the economy more than $454 billion in lost productivity each year.
- 42.1 million people still smoke.
- According to Distraction.gov, at any given moment, 660,000 drivers are on their cell phones or manipulating some sort of electronic device amounting to more than 23 trillion distractions each day.
- 63 percent of Americans don't get the sleep they need; of those, 95 percent surf the net, watch TV, text, or engage in social media in the hour before they go to sleep.
- On average, Americans spend four and a half hours per day watching TV and another 4 and half hours texting, emailing, messaging and surfing the net.

No one has said that life is easy, but why do people insist on making it harder when, with a little effort and determination, they can make exponential gains through incremental changes? However, admittedly, even that is not so easy without some help. Trying to change our behavior while we're racing through life is like trying to retrofit a 747 aircraft while it's flying in the air. But, it can be done; we just need a blueprint – a foolproof guide that allows us to make painless, incremental changes that become behavioral fixtures on the run. That's where the 80/20 Rule for Living comes in. It's simple, effective and it can be applied to just about any aspect of your life in which you're seeking positive change.

The 80/20 Power Hour

A great place to start applying the 80/20 rule is in your schedule. For each of us, there is at least one hour during the day when we are most energetic, most effective and the least distracted. It may be your first walking hour, or it may be the hour after you exercise; whenever it is, you need to block that hour to perform the most challenging activities and address you're most important priorities. This almost guarantees that the best 20 percent of your day will produce outsized results concentrating on the most vital issues on your list. You'll be amazed that you can accomplish more in an all-out, one hour sprint than you can in the remaining 80 percent of your day.

Of course, this presumes that you first clearly identify your most important tasks and top priorities, leaving non-essential or non-urgent activities for the rest of your schedule.

Bonus Tip: If you can increase the length of your "power hour" by 20 percent (adding 10 minutes at a time), you will increase the amount of your productive time and your output will expand exponentially.

The 80/20 Dieting Plan

Most reasonable people would agree that most diets are simply fads that pad the wallets of their promoters with no long term benefit for the dieter. Your diet is nothing more than the cumulative results of your eating habits; and any activity rooted in habits requires behavioral adjustments. Although most diets are based on changing behavior, most are so radical in their changes that most people can't tolerate them for any length of time.

Rather than starting a new diet that has high expectations and questionable results, it might be better to simply take a new approach to healthier eating. Weight control is typically a by-product of healthier eating with the primary benefits of more energy, better moods, stronger immunity, lower stress and slower aging.

A good example is the habit of eating a high sugar, carb-loaded breakfast in the morning. We know that eating high sugary foods leads to a spike in our blood level which forces the body to release more insulin. Although we may feel a surge of energy, it's typically only temporary and usually leads to an energy crash around mid-morning. Because the body demands more sugar to keep our energy level up, we often comply by loading up on carb-laden lunch. Of course, that leads to the afternoon energy crash that leaves us tired and wanting.

Out of an eight hour work day, we might get three to four hours of high productivity. Almost certainly our mood is soured and the stress of lower productivity makes us more vulnerable to ills such as headaches or the feeling of "I'd rather be anywhere right now than here" – not exactly the healthiest disposition.

Who wants to feel that way? But the critical first step to change is to recognize the habits that lead to that outcome. What if, instead, you had a breakfast low sugar, protein-rich breakfast, such as a veggie/ham and cheese/egg sandwich on high fiber bread? You would be far less likely to go on a blood sugar roller coaster and you would feel fuller longer. By adding a healthy, mid-morning snack, such as fruit or yogurt, you would approach lunch only needing to sustain your energy level, not having to revive it. You would eat less, and, you could focus on healthier selections. Add another healthy mid-afternoon snack, such as raisins and nuts, and you end the day at the same level of energy and alertness as when you started.

Here's how to apply the 80/20 principle to changing your eating behavior.

The first critical step is to recognize that it is very difficult to make a 180 degree turn on a dime. So, rather than completely cleaning out your refrigerator and pantry, begin to gradually replace those foods that reinforce unhealthy eating, with healthier choices. It would help to do some research and plan menus so you know what you need to buy on your future trips to the grocery store.

Your goal each day should be to eat just 80 percent of what you ate the day before that wouldn't be considered a healthy choice, and replace the 20 percent with healthier choices. Each day you accomplish this, you progressively replace an increasing amount of your unhealthy choices with healthy choices. The ideal objective would be to have 80 percent of your diet consist of healthy choices and only 20 percent less healthy choices. If you can achieve that, the 20 percent you consume in less healthy choices can be viewed as your "cheat" meals.

Bonus Tip: While you are applying the 80/20 principle to healthier eating, you could also apply it to your food consumption. Try shaving your portions by 20 percent to the point when you're just 80 percent full; then replace it with a healthy liquid, such as water or non-sugary juice.

The 80/20 Plan to Eliminate the Bad Five C's of Life

It's generally found that, when we allow our behavior to be overwhelmed by bad habits, we are more likely to dwell in the world of the Bad Five C's – Chaos, Confusion, Conflict, Clutter and Complaining. And, when that happens, it doesn't take an outside observer to tell us how unproductive, emotionally strained, and physically drained we become in that state. We can feel it and see it, and it's reflected in our daily outcomes – poor work performance, procrastinating important activities or decisions, deteriorating relationships, sleepless nights, and a lack of energy.

No one wants to consciously live in that world, but, for many people it's either all they've known or they simply lack the control mechanisms to alter their lives. That's where the 80/20 principle can help – by incrementally increasing the amount of control you have in your life and systematically changing your course.

If we apply the basic 80/20 principle to our lives, we can assume that, for the average person, 20 percent of our input during the day generates 80 percent of our positive output. That means the other 80 percent of our input is generating either negative output or no output at all. What are the sources of that "wasted" input? It could be inactivity (i.e., watching TV, sleeping too long, etc.), or unconscious activity (daydreaming, surfing the net, playing video games, unhealthy or excessive eating, etc.) As, previously applied to healthy eating, the 80/20 principle seeks to incrementally reduce the negative input with positive input which will expand the amount of positive output we create.

When viewed in through the scope of a 24-hour day in which we are allotted eight hours of sleep to prepare for eight hours of work, and we spend only 20 percent of the remaining eight hours in generating positive output, then what are we doing during the other 6.4 hours, and how is that affecting our lives?

Consider this short poem I composed on to illustrate the answer:

To Begin, I press the snooze button thrice
Sit up; roll my eyes, as sleep didn't suffice.
Go back to Bed and lay down again
To wake up and realize I am late and insane

I brush – actually, gargle the pastes
Eyes closed in shower, when opened, feel disgraced

I drive in a hurry, cut through lanes in panic
Look in Rear view mirror, my face looks satanic

In hope of recovery, gulp my daily pills
Slides thereafter on passenger seat, the stack of bills
Slam my brakes, for I didn't see the car ahead
Saved by the inch, or I would have been dead

My shirt crumbled and pants full of crease
Rush to park, just to step on grease
Walk with grease marks all over
Rub my shoes non-stop on mat, oh what a disaster

On my desk, my head down and disengaged
Phone rings I don't hear, boss and team enraged
Facebook, twitter posts driving me crazy
Sleeplessness making desk look hazy

Starving, I eat junk and my stomach bloats
Go to my desk and see it flooded with notes
Notes of work that I was supposed to complete
Its 5 and I stay late to do and not feel defeat

Driving back screaming to my bickering wife
She says I have no life
Either I change course today.
She stops and says she will have me divorced any way

Drive home with eyes half open, counting on night lights
Follow cars at every sight
Cops pass by, causing me a plight
I never get my day quite right

Starving and eat junk again
My stomach bloats and is in pain
Enter my home through the back door like a thief
Oh I am in so much grief.

Dive on the couch and Sleep in vain
Hoping I never wake up again.
This is not the Life I need
Get me the change I always want, just to Succeed.

How many "bad" habits did you count? If you were going to change the course of this day, where would you start? How would you apply the 80/20 principle? The poem began with, "*I press the snooze button thrice,*" which didn't suffice, and, it seems, everything snowballed from there.

Is it conceivable that, if I were able to jump up without hitting the snooze button, things might have gone at least a little different? But, must be a reason why I couldn't. Obviously, I wasn't fully rested. But why? The answer is not likely to be found in any one behavior, habit or activity – it's more likely a result of a combination of things, and their cumulative effect over time. However, if I could choose just one, today, to start changing my course, what would it be and how would I change it?

Let's go back to the beginning of the day. What if I decide to change my habit of hitting the snooze button three times? I could probably will myself to turn off the alarm tomorrow and drag myself out of bed. But, would I be able to do it the next day, and the day after that. In changing a behavior, one as ingrained as hitting the snooze button every day, it could be more effective to change incrementally. Rather than going cold turkey and not hitting it all tomorrow, I will only hit it twice (instead of three times). Once I begin to realize the positive results of waking up 15 minutes earlier, I can then increase the positive input by hitting it one less time.

Conceivably, by targeting the good behavior of waking up on time, it can create a cascade effect on other desirable behaviors, such as – eating a healthier breakfast, driving sensibly to get to work on time, better appearance and mood, being more productive, and more energized to exercise which can lead to healthier eating at dinner and better sleep at night.

Here is list of 20 behaviors that emphasize the Good Five C's of Life. Targeting just one at a time will have a compounding effect on how you live your life:

1. Waking up early or on time
2. Driving sensibly
3. Exercising for 30 minutes or more daily or 4 times a week.
4. Sleeping for Seven Hours Daily
5. Counting 1 to 10 in 2 second increments when angry
6. Working more on important but not urgent tasks daily
7. Preparing and planning for your day everyday

8. Working majority of the daily work tasks in my unique ability

9. Spending undivided time and attention for one hour daily with kids

10. No working or travel on Sundays

11. Being in bed no later than 10:30 PM at night

12. No exposure to TV or to any sort of electronic devices or screens for one hour before I go to sleep

13. Taking a shower before I go to bed (really helps you get a sound sleep at night – go to sleep with a fresh mind)

14. Never miss an event involving my children

15. Reading for 30 minutes a day 3-4 times a week.

16. Allow for prayer or meditation before going to sleep

17. Offering a prayer of gratitude before eating

18. Drinking 8 glasses of water daily

19. Expanding my knowledge, experience and resources at least twice per week

20. Eating only 80 percent of my meals or snacks or in-between meals everyday

The key is to focus on one at a time, have an action plan for changing it and, as you achieve success with it, assess its effect on other behaviors. Then, target another behavior with a specific plan to change and track your progress.

An Important Word about Sleep

You may have noticed the mention of sleep habits a few times throughout this book – and with good reason. It has been scientifically documented that sleep – or the lack thereof – has a profound impact on our ability to function, to reason and, ultimately, on our longevity. Countless studies have found a link between insufficient sleep and some serious health problems, such as heart disease, heart attacks, diabetes, and obesity, any of which can cut your life short.

Then there's the shocking statistic from the Institute of Medicine which estimates that one out of five auto accidents in the U.S. results from drowsy driving – that's about 1 million crashes a year. If you really want to lay awake at night, consider that nearly half of licensed drivers in the U.S. (of which there are 211,000,000), have actually fallen asleep at the wheel, if even for a split second. Do you count yourself among them?

Clearly, poor sleep habits can be life-threatening; however, the inattention to the amount and quality of sleep we get each night can affect our quality of life, and, ultimately, our state of happiness.

We know, for example, that when we don't get enough sleep we're more likely to be cranky, over-reactive, and sometimes hysterical if we're extremely overtired. As a result, our mood can send us into depression and our relationships suffer.

When we're exhausted from lack of sleep, we are more likely to forego exercise due to a lack of energy; or we are less likely to feel up to cooking a healthy dinner. There is a direct correlation between sleep loss and weight gain.

Even more far-reaching, sleep loss affects how we think. It impairs our cognition, which we rely on to be able to focus and make decisions. Sleep deprived people are generally much worse at problem-solving than well-rested people; and they're more prone to forgetfulness.

Who really wants to live like that, considering we have a choice in the matter? We all know some "morning people" – those people who seem to leap out of bed early and, somehow, maintain a cheery disposition from dusk to dawn. They can be especially irritating to people who live in a sleep-deprived state of exhaustion and crankiness. But, "morning people" benefit from more than just cheerfulness. The science backs up the notion that they are also healthier and much more productive. Consider the research:

They earn better grades – In a 2008 Texas University study, college students who identified themselves as "morning people" earned a full point higher on their GPAs than those who were "night owls" (3.5 vs. 2.5). Good grades help students' secure better career opportunities.

They are more proactive –Harvard biologist Christoph Randler discovered in 2008 that early risers are more proactive. They were more likely to agree with statements like "I spend time identifying long-range goals for myself" and "I feel in charge of making things happen."

They anticipate problems – Randler's research also revealed that "morning people" are more likely to anticipate problems and minimize them efficiently, which leads to more success in the business world.

They are more optimistic – Various studies have shown that morning people exhibit character traits like optimism, being agreeable, satisfaction and conscientiousness. Night owls, while linked with creativity and intelligence, are more likely to exhibit traits like depression, pessimism and being neurotic.

They get quality sleep – Sleep experts say that if you go to bed earlier and wake up earlier, your body will be more in tune with the earth's circadian rhythms, which offers more restorative sleep.

The 80/20 principle can be especially effective in incrementally adjusting your sleeping pattern. By reducing poor lifestyle choices – i.e. staying up too late; eating too late; watching TV or surfing the net just before bedtime; drinking alcohol late at night; failing to exercise; not having a game plan for the next day; etc. – by 20 percent each day or week, you will increase your ability to enjoy a better sleep by 80 percent. It's about lifestyle choices and the determination to vastly improve the quality of your life.

Applying the 80/20 Principle to Your Unique Ability

I'm going to make a remarkable claim right here; and that is, if you were able to spend 80 percent of your time exercising your Unique Ability®, you would be happier and self-fulfilled 100 percent of the time. You'll recall from Chapter 6 (Simplifying Business Decisions), that the Unique Ability® is a concept created by renowned development coach, Dan Sullivan, which stresses the unrelenting pursuit of identifying, developing and cultivating your Unique Ability® – that special talent or skill about which you are passionate and that you can do exceptionally well.

As Dan has been able to demonstrate, without exception, each of us has an incredible force within us – a talent, a skill or a passion – that has yet to be fully utilized; and, when we find a way to harness and develop it, it can transform our own life as well as the lives of people around us. It's an ability about which we are so incredibly passionate, we will find ways to exercise it as much as possible and work to improve it to the extent that it becomes your life's purpose.

It's astounding, but not so surprising, that more than 80 percent of the American population spends the vast majority of their time in work they don't enjoy. Needless to say, they are nowhere in the sphere of achieving happiness and fulfillment. Most people are trapped in a vicious cycle of dependency on others to create their happiness for them, not realizing that, by taking a few minutes to focus on something that impassions them or makes them truly unique, they can begin the process of developing their Unique Ability. And, if they can incorporate their Unique Ability in their work, it no longer has to be "work," but, rather, something you love doing every day.

I'm a financial advisor by training and profession; however, I am passionate about helping people to become high achievers in life and in business. I love creating processes that people can use to systematically transform their core essentials to be able to make more effective decisions that contribute to their own pursuit of happiness. Because I am advising people regarding their finances, I am able to impart many aspects of my passion in helping them better manage their financial lives. In essence, I am exercising my Unique Ability every day.

The goal is to create a plan that will lead you to a life in which you will be able to spend at least 80 percent of your time in your Unique Ability, 80 percent at a time. So, if you start out only being able to spend 20 percent of your time in your Unique Ability, find a way to increase that time by 80 percent to 30 percent. The increased happiness, energy and fulfillment you'll realize with each incremental increase in time, will provide the motivation to keep going. Your addiction to your Unique Ability will provide the fuel to keep moving forward.

The first challenge is finding your Unique Ability, and the second challenge is in finding ways to expand the amount of time you can exercise it. I recommend Dan Sullivan's book, *Unique Ability®: Creating the Life You Want,* to anyone who wants to discover and develop their Unique Ability and transform their lives.

The 80/20 Tracker™ Mobile Application

The 80/20 Tracker™ Mobile Application, available as in-app purchase from The Decision Simplifier™ application, is designed to help you achieve an 80 percent result with 20 percent effort. As outlined in this chapter, the impact of the 80 percent approach in our life can enable us to achieve success and milestones much sooner than we could have imagined. So it is important to blend the 80/20 rule into your life whenever a significant change is required.

As with the other "coaching" apps we offer, such as the Decision Simplifier™, and the Happiness Helper™, the 80/20 Tracker™ app is not designed to give you the answers you need – only you can provide those. Rather, it's designed to ask you the right questions, the tough questions that others won't ask of you, or you won't ask of yourself. Ultimately, you have to decide which choice to make or action to take; however, based on your answers, the application will guide you through the process of taking the actions you need to form a new habit.

Systems to implement as a habit when applicable to your situation:

I. Developing your "Power Hour"
    1. Through the workshop, determine the hidden essential drivers that can transform your day in one hour and help you do more in one hour that what you do in a day.
    2. Discover the activities that you need to build to make that quantum leap in your life in one year.
    3. Implement those on a daily basis.

Do more in one hour than many others with The Power Hour™ workshop at http://www.BizActionCoach.com/product/the-power-hour/

II. The 80/20 Diet Plan:
    1. Through the workshop, discover the easy 80/20 system I used to go from 230 lbs to 165 lbs.
    2. From the workshop, find the hidden ways to build new habits to change your diet.
    3. Apply those habits for 21 days.

Control your diet with The 80/20 Diet™ workshop at http://www.BizActionCoach.com/pre-recorded-workshops/

III. The 80/20 Revenue Plan:
   1. Build a list or find out how many clients (starting with the biggest) did it take to get to 80 percent of revenues.
   2. What percentage does that represent of your overall client source?
   3. Through the workshop, discover the hidden strategies that you need to build upon in your business to multiply your biggest clients.

Make more money with less clients with The 80/20 Revenue™ workshop at http://www.BizActionCoach.com/pre-recorded-workshops/

IV. The 80/20 Productivity Plan:
   1. Through the workshop, discover the secret of how by using the 80/20 productivity system we launched the 52 workshops and 52 deck of cards system in less than 52 days.
   2. From the workshop, find the hidden ways to delegate or systematize and reduce your core activities to a minimum.
   3. Put a deadline date and implement the same.

Get more done in less time with less with The 80/20 Productivity Plan™ workshop at http://www.BizActionCoach.com/product/the-8020-productivity/

V. The 80/20 Exercise plan:
1. Through the workshop, discover the hidden ways of how I achieved more results in less time by using the 80/20 exercise routine.
2. Build the list of activities you need to do and improvise them.
3. Implement the same for 21 days and write those dates.

Improve your daily exercise with The 80/20 Exercise™ Workshop   http://www.BizActionCoach.com/product/the-8020-exercise/

VI. The Sleep Formula™:
1. Write down all your current obstacles that is preventing you from getting a sound sleep
2. From the workshop, discover the secret strategies you need to implement overcome those obstacles.
3. Watch the workshop to find hidden ways to create a "Sleep Ritual."
4. Implement your sleep ritual for 21 days.

Sleep better with The Sleep Formula™ workshop at http://www.BizActionCoach.com/product/the-sleep-formula/
To buy The Sleep Formula™ DVD, please visit www.BizActionCoach.com/DVD/

Get the entire deck of cards (52 Cards-52 Systems) at http://www.BizActionCoach.com/product/the-deck-of-cards-workshop-system/

Chapter Workbook Exercises

Establish your power hour for accomplishing your most important tasks of the day

- Determine which hour you are at your most alert and most energetic
- Prioritize your tasks by importance (not urgency)
- Spend your power hour focused on these tasks, working on one at a time
- Keep a journal of your accomplishments for each power hour

Start your 80/20 healthy eating plan

- Identify those foods you want to reduce or eliminate from your diet for each meal of the day
- Create a list of healthy alternatives you know you will be able to prepare
- Focus on reducing your intake of healthy choices by 20 percent each day until 80 percent of your meals are comprised of healthy food choices.
- Include in your grocery shopping list healthy snack choices for between meals
- Keep a food journal to track your progress.

Target and prioritize five behaviors you want to change

- Working on one at a time, describe the behavior and why it may be causing chaos, clutter, confusion or conflict in your life.
- Now describe the counter behavior you wish to achieve and how that would help reduce or eliminate any of the Bad Five C's.
- List a minimum of three specific action steps you need to take each day to consciously create the habit that will change the behavior and perform them daily for at least 28 days.
- Rinse and repeat for the next targeted behavior.

Begin to develop your Unique Ability

- Take a quiet moment to think about something you love to do – a special talent or skill you feel passionate about.
- Determine how much time you can devote to your special talent or skill each day or week and build that into your schedule.
- As you plan each day or week, find a way to increase the amount of time you can devote to your Unique Ability by 20 percent.
- If you're absolutely serious about spending most of your time in your Unique Ability, buy Dan Sullivan's book, *Unique Ability®: Creating the Life You Want,* and schedule at least three hours a week to following his process.

Please complete the exercise on the next page before proceeding to read the next chapter.

What thought or thoughts come to your mind after reading this chapter?

_____

_____

_____

_____

_____

_____

_____

What Decision or Decisions have you made about the thought or thoughts you had?

_____

_____

_____

_____

_____

_____

_____

What Growth Actions would you take today or by a specific date to implement your thoughts?

_____

_____

_____

_____

_____

_____

_____

A True Story

I lost more than 50 lbs. by applying the 80/20 rule in my life to my health. I cut down my diet to 80 percent of what I was eating before and started eating in smaller plates. I combined that with at least 5 of 7 days of cardio and strength exercises. This routine helped me get in shape and lose 6 inches. I apply the 80/20 rule every day to my tasks and activities to get done and get far more leverage. This book wouldn't have been possible without the 80/20 approach. Many of you might shy away from taking on big and bold projects because of the amount of time, commitment and resources you feel might have to devote. I did it by getting it in motion and getting it started.

Chapter 8

for a better life, follow the principles of happiness

Living the Principles of Happiness

i f achieving life happiness was easy then everyone would be happy, wouldn't they? If it were as simple as choosing to be happy, why would anyone choose to be unhappy? If we knew every decision we make would lead us further down our happiness path, what need would there be for seeking advice, second opinions or other options? While these questions invite simple, obvious answers, when they're placed in the context of today's realities, they're not very serious questions. Of course, everyone would like to be happy; and nobody, except perhaps, the stubborn among us, chooses to be unhappy.

In reality though, life happens; it constantly throws us curves and serves up lemons. For even the most optimistic among us, things don't always work out for the best. All the positive thinking in the world cannot prevent bad things from happening, no matter how much lemonade you can make. Let's face it, sustained happiness is hard. And, trying too hard to be happy can make you unhappy, especially when a relentless focus on it simply brings out all the ways you aren't happy. Discouraging? It can be. Hopeless? Not at all; but remember, hope is not a strategy.

That's why you have this book. It's full of strategies and tactics to overcome the obstacles to happiness. It refocuses your energy on building the traits and habits that can lead you confidently down your happiness path. With each habit or trait learned, your natural inclination evolves, turning you towards the positive and away from discouragement. It's not easy. Anything so worthwhile never is. But it can be done. And the reward of lifetime fulfillment will trump any other possible achievement.

It's a conscious choice to pick up this book and follow through each day to build the habits to happiness and develop the tools to simplify your decision-making for leading a more productive life. But, there will be setbacks; lots of them. The true test of your development will be how you cope with them; and how quickly you can convert mistakes and failure into the energy that propels you forward.

When you are overcome with a wave of discouragement or despair, there is one, simple antidote that will keep you on course. It takes just a few minutes; but it's very powerful –

meditation or prayer. And, if you're wondering what it is you should mediate or pray about, let me suggest you share your gratitude for the things you do have; for the moments of happiness you've enjoyed today. Because, until you recognize all of the reasons to be happy today, there can be no assurance that anything will bring you happiness tomorrow. You will always want more, and that can never bring life happiness.

Alternatively, if you hitch your lifestyle choices and financial decisions to a set of principles, grounded in deeply rooted values and beliefs, you will more readily find contentment. What do I mean by principles? Principles are a fundamental truth or tenets that serve as a foundation for a system of belief, or for a chain of reasoning. In other words, they serve as a guide for making decisions that keep you aligned with your values and beliefs.

What are Your Principles of Life?

For centuries, philosophers, worldly thinkers and all of the various religions have proposed fundamental principles of life. Judeo-Christian principles are based in the Ten Commandments and biblical teachings, and followers of the Buddhism and Hindu religions are steeped in their ancient philosophies. Non-religious people look to innumerable non-sectarian sources for principles to follow, such as the Hawaiian Huna, or "The Secret" Laws of Attraction. The common bond shared by these sources of principles is the abiding faith their followers have in the underlying values and beliefs that form their foundations. They are also linked by their central focus on the power of the individual to live a life of fulfillment and happiness.

Ultimately, it is your life experiences that will shape your principles, refined by your own values and beliefs. The key is to clearly define them, articulate them (write them down and share them), and then place your faith in them as your steady guide to living a life of fulfillment. By strictly adhering to your principles of life, whatever they may be, your daily life will be far less chaotic and cluttered, and that will translate into more clarity and conviction in your daily decisions, large and small.

And, whether you want to use them as an example for establishing your own principles, or feel they are a match for your own values and beliefs; I commend them to you here:

Uniqueness – each of us have an incredible force within us, comprised of our personal talents, passions and skills. God have given us this unique ability which is just waiting to be discovered, nurtured and utilized for the betterment of ourselves and the world around us. When we can use our unique ability in our daily lives, we are firmly on the path to life happiness.

Truth – living with integrity requires that we maintain alignment with our values and beliefs, which means being honest with ourselves about who we are and what we need in life; and being honest with others in all of our dealings with people.

Respect – without self-respect there can be no self-discipline; and without respect of others there can be no self-respect. Without self-discipline, there is no control over right and wrong.

Responsibility – all of us arrived on this Earth with the gifts of time and talents with an expectation that we will use them for the betterment of all, especially those in need.

Simplicity – clarity, one of the keys to happiness, comes through simplicity. Sophistication and elegance comes through simplicity.

Value self over possessions – people who define themselves by their possessions will never be happy because they will never have enough. People should accept the truth of how they can achieve fulfillment by developing their positive traits and unique abilities.

Collaboration—there is nothing more powerful than the collective mind. No one can possibly know all he or she needs to know in significant matters, so it is foolish to try to go it alone. There's just too much at stake. Seek the counsel and advice of experts in matters of career, finances, and relationships.

Whether you want to design your own principles of life, or adopt the established principles of your faith or other belief system, it must come down to having clarity in your own beliefs and values. More importantly, it needs to be placed in the context of a larger purpose – one that encompasses your own ambition for a good life and its imprint on the world around you. That will be your North Star.

If it is to Be, It is up to Thee

You've come a long way in this brief, and hopefully, enlightening journey – all the way from discovering your path to happiness to learning the ways in which simplifying your decision-making can propel you down the path. And, yes, it is a journey, which means it doesn't end here. Each day brings the challenge of staying true to your purpose and keeping your actions and decisions aligned with your principles. Your work has just begun. And, yes, it is work, especially if you are new to it. But, hopefully, the steps outlined in this book along with the simple chapter exercises will help you form the critical habits that will propel you down the path, effortlessly and deliberately.

Remember, when you love what you do, it's not really work; that's true of your job, and it's true of your own personal development (for the love of self). Whether you are set on improving your productivity, becoming a high achiever, or simply finding genuine happiness, you now have the tools and know the steps to properly gain control of your destiny. As with any method or process, you need to practice it; utilize it; share it; teach it; and then you will love it for what it can do for you as well as for those you love.

I leave you with one last exercise. It could be the most important habit you develop. People trying to quit smoking sometimes wear a rubber band on their wrist which they snap when they feel a moment of weakness.

If, in your efforts to stay the course in your pursuit of happiness, you start to falter or lose your way, just snap out a good thought.

"A good Thought leads to good Words, to good Habits, to good Deeds, to a good character, and, ultimately, to a Great Destiny."

—Mahatma Gandhi.

Systems to implement as a habit when applicable to your situation:

I. Developing your "Principles of Happiness"
    1. Through the workshop, discover the hidden ways to build a list of activities to help you practice your principles of happiness every day.
    2. Put deadlines and/or dates of when you are implementing the same.
    3. Continue the exercise for 21 days until it becomes a habit.

Happily lead with your principles with The Principles of Happiness™ workshop at http://www.BizActionCoach.com/product/the-principles-of-happiness/

II. Building your Uniqueness:
    1. Through the workshop, discover the hidden ways to capitalize your talent.
    2. Build the 10 ways you will be different from your competition in your passionate activities.
    3. Find out the habits you need to remove, add and change and implement the same for 21 days.

Become a dominator in your work or business with The Only You™ workshop at http://www.BizActionCoach.com/product/the-only-you/

III. The Confidence Implementor:
1. From the workshop, discover the hidden steps to build your confidence on a daily basis.
2. Find the triggers that raise or decrease your confidence on a daily basis and through the workshop find the secret on how to deal with those triggers successfully every day.
3. Discover and build the habits and discipline you need to build your confidence on a daily basis and do it for 21 days until it has become a habit.

Improve your confidence level with The Confidence Implementor™ workshop at http://www.BizActionCoach.com/product/the-confidence-builder/

IV. The Belief Cleanser™
1. From the workshop, discover how to overcome the beliefs that hamper our progress and build upon the beliefs that aid our progress.
2. Find the hidden secret on how to develop beliefs that connect to your goals and develop a list of activities, habits, and discipline you need for the same.
3. Implement the same for 21 days.

Clean the beliefs that hamper your growth with The Belief Cleanser™ workshop at http://www.BizActionCoach.com/product/the-belief-cleanser/

V. The Self Discovery:
   1. Tell the truth to yourself about yourself. Go stand up in front of a full length mirror and stare at yourself for 2 full minutes.
   2. From the workshop, discover the secret on how to overcome the truths about yourself that are hampering your progress.
   3. Discover the hidden ways to make you implement the discipline your need to overcome the challenges you face about yourself.
   4. Take the first step by implementing at least one of those right away.

Discover your true self The Self Discovery™ Workshop at http://www.BizActionCoach.com/product/the-self-discovery/

VI. The Good Thought Snap:
   1. Whenever you are feeling stressed, snap your fingers and clear your mind.
   2. Discover the secret ways to relieve your stress by disconnecting and connecting to what's essential at the moment.
   3. Through the workshop, find hidden ways to recreate great memories. Snap your fingers again.

Relieve stress in a snap with The Good Thought Snap™ workshop at http://www.BizActionCoach.com/product/the-good-thought-snap/

VII. The Responsibility Enhancer™:
1. Write down the top three responsibilities that you want to take but never found the time to do so.
2. From the workshop, discover the steps you need to take to overcome the challenges that are preventing you from taking that responsibility.
3. Write down dates and times you will implement the first one to three steps for taking on that additional responsibility.

Easily take on more responsibilities with The Responsibility Enhancer™ Workshop at http://www.BizActionCoach.com/product/the-responsibility-enhancer/

VIII. The Collaboration Maximizer™:
1. Write down one to three things you absolutely can't figure out how to do it yourself and wish you had someone help you do it.
2. From the workshop, discover the hidden ways to build joint ventures and collaboration that requires the least out of pocket expense for you.
3. With the aid of the tools in the workshop, build a list of steps and strategies you need to execute to maximize your collaboration.
4. Implement at least one of the steps in the next 24 hours.

Effectively collaborate with The Collaboration Maximizer™ workshop at http://www.BizActionCoach.com/product/the-collaboration-maximizer/

Get the entire deck of cards (52 Cards-52 Systems) at http://www.BizActionCoach.com/product/the-deck-of-cards-workshop-system/

Resources:

Website: www.BizActionCoach.com

Financial Calculators: http://www.BizActionCoach.com/financial-calculators/

12 Daily Tools DIY Systems: We have boldly created incredibly powerful resources for you.

Please visit the DIY page http://www.BizActionCoach.com/dvd/ on our website and check these out:

1. The 80/20 Transformation™
2. The Daily Goal Achiever™
3. The Daily Goal Setter™
4. The Daily Effort Transformer™
5. The Friction Destroyer™
6. The Interruption Eliminator™
7. The Deal Sealer™
8. The Opinion Builder™
9. The Team Process™
10. The Plan Aligner™
11. The Sleep Formula™
12. The Appointment Maker™

Mobile Application: Download "Rajparth" for free on your droid or apple phone. Future in-app purchases to arrive soon as follows:

1. The Decision Simplifier™
2. The 80-20 Tracker™
3. The Happiness Multiplier™

Online Course:
www.TheDecisionSimplifier.com
A robust online course to make decision making easy.

You Tube Channel:
"High Achiever Success Systems"
https://www.youtube.com/channel/UC_
wrH36CwIGcr5aHbVPyYWA

Podcast: I love Progress (ITunes and Droid)
ITunes: I Love Progress
https://itunes.apple.com/us/podcast/i-love-progress
/id1017127647?mt=2&inf_contact_key=be711fd4c
0665435076f625695ecb3ec0ca32bdbf2c46efba
40f7d6ba4edf193

Droid or any other device or computer:
http://www.BizActionCoach.com/podcasts/

about the author

*Bimal Shah—Author
and Ami Shah—Editor*

Bimal Shah is well-known in South Florida and in business community for the last 17 years. Bimal is on a die-hard mission to provide Security from enemies of prosperity and build high achievers throughout the world. He does it by building and maintaining customized systems of coaching, planning and achieving. He is a recognized speaker with presentations at several professional business associations, conferences, and meetings. He is a lifetime member of Million Dollar Round Table®, MDRT. He is also a member of Top of the Table®, Million Dollar Round Table®, the highest level of recognition in the financial services industry. Bimal has been a Top of the Table® member consecutively for the last 6 years.

He has been awarded the Global Corporate Award in 2014 for being the best in the world in the life insurance category. Bimal's organization helps bring control and charge in the lives of entrepreneurs by making their teams happily engaged, striking a balance between Work and Life, adding security from the Seven enemies of Wealth, and making their business very unique and different from the competitors. Bimal's organization also helps business owners and professionals improve their present situation and build a favorable financial future. Bimal lives with his wife Ami and two kids in the Boca Raton area. His Hobbies include Horse Riding and Reading.

claim your bonus

As an entrepreneur, you go through many challenges, pains, and frustrations. It is difficult, disappointing, and disheartening at times. I know it, I have lived it for 17 years. There's hasn't been a single year where the journey wasn't filled with obstacles that many a times seemed impossible to deal with. I have overcome all of them with the strong support of my family and my team. Without a doubt, I can tell you that building a team around you is essential.

As a bonus, I am going to give you this comprehensive report that will show you how to build a strong employee retention as a business owner or if you are just building a team around you, how to build a great team.

This $99 value is your gift for investing in *The Daily Happiness Multiplier.*

Claim it by going to http://bit.ly/1WCQAqx

If you would like to qualify for a $999 Live Workshop at no cost to you, please go to http://bit.ly/1FNJN94

If you qualify and are selected, this $999 gift is yours for investing in the book.

important QR codes

Scan this QR Code to Start
Your Success For FREE.

Scan this QR Code to
download Bimal's V-Card

Scan this QR Code to
Discover even more on
the 52 Secrets.

Scan this QR Code to **Get**
the entire 52 Secrets System

Scan this QR Code to
download our Smartphone
App for FREE

Scan this QR Code to qualify
for a FREE Live Interactive
Workshop.